Scripture Discussion Commentary 1

P9-DWJ-119

SCRIPTURE DISCUSSION COMMENTARY 1

Series editor: Laurence Bright

Pentateuch

Genesis 1-11	*Joseph Blenkinsopp*
Genesis 12-50	*Joseph Blenkinsopp*
Exodus	*John Challenor*
Deuteronomy	*Joseph Blenkinsopp*

ACTA Foundation
Adult Catechetical Teaching Aids
Chicago, Illinois

First published 1971
ACTA Foundation (Adult Catechetical Teaching Aids),
4848 N. Clark Street, Chicago, Illinois 60640
© 1971 Joseph Blenkinsopp, John Challenor

Nihil obstat : John M. T. Barton STD LSS *Censor*
Imprimatur : + Victor Guazzelli *Vicar General*
Westminster, 21 June 1971

2538

Library of Congress number 71–173033

ISBN 0 87946 000 8

Made and printed in Great Britain by
William Clowes & Sons, Limited
London, Beccles and Colchester

Contents

General Introduction

A few of the individual units which make up this series of biblical commentaries have already proved their worth issued as separate booklets. Together with many others they are now grouped together in a set of twelve volumes covering almost all the books of the old and new testaments—a few have been omitted as unsuitable to the general purpose of the series.

That purpose is primarily to promote discussion. This is how these commentaries differ from the others that exist. They do not cover all that could be said about the biblical text, but concentrate on the features most likely to get lively conversation going—those, for instance, with special relevance for later developments of thought, or for life in the church and world of today. For this reason passages of narrative are punctuated by sets of questions designed to get a group talking, though the text of scripture, helped by the remarks of the commentator, should have already done just that.

For the text is what matters. Individuals getting ready for a meeting, the group itself as it meets, should always have the bible centrally present, and use the commentary only as a tool. The bibliographies will help those wishing to dig deeper.

What kinds of group can work in this way? Absolutely

viii General Introduction

any. The bible has the reputation of being difficult, and in some respects it is, but practice quickly clears up a lot of initial obstacles. So parish groups of any kind can and should be working on it. The groups needn't necessarily already exist, it is enough to have a few like-minded friends and to care sufficiently about finding out what the bible means. Nor need they be very large; one family could be quite enough. High schools (particularly in the senior year), colleges and universities are also obvious places for groups to form. If possible they should everywhere be ecumenical in composition: though all the authors are Roman catholics, there is nothing sectarian in their approach.

In each volume there are two to four, or occasionally more, studies of related biblical books. Each one is self-contained; it is neither necessary nor desirable to start at the beginning and plough steadily through. Take up, each time, what most interests you—there is very little in scripture that is actually dull! Since the commentaries are by different authors, you will discover differences of outlook, in itself a matter for discussion. Above all, remember that getting the right general approach to reading the bible is more important than answering any particular question about the text—and that this approach only comes with practice.

LAURENCE BRIGHT

Genesis 1–11

Joseph Blenkinsopp

Introduction

The first part of Genesis being a particularly well devised trap for the unwary, the following brief remarks are offered as a help towards creating the right kind of awareness before starting to read. We may add that the very brevity of this section—less than a third of the length of this small commentary—should make it easier to get really close to the text.

First, why read the old testament at all? Since it deals with fundamental human problems—creation, human origins, sex, sin and death—it will have even for the uncommitted reader at least as much significance as, say, Plato's *Dialogues*. It offers, among other things, a kind of diagnosis of the human situation focused on one historical community. This aspect should not be underplayed even by the christian reader, and perhaps we should give it some thought before going on to use words like 'redemption', 'salvation history', and the like. Diagnosis is surely a necessary element in salvation. however we define this latter. Take a mentally sick person who goes to a psychiatrist in search of 'salvation'. The psychiatrist cannot speak the liberating word until he has made the patient understand his present situation in the context of a total personal history. Salvation is not identical with diagnosis but is somehow present within it. We christians talk a lot about salvation and redemption, but our lives are often riddled with fear, insecurity, and guilt which we

unconsciously work off on other people. The suggestion
here is that the old testament, especially the part we are
going to study, is a kind of diagnosis. Gen 1–11 belong far
less to the category of history than to that of wisdom
writing. Of course, the diagnosis is not just personal but
collective, a scanning by Israel of the totality of her history and experience in the world—a kind of group
therapy. And the christian both culturally and spiritually
is part of that history and experience.

Of course, the christian conviction is that God revealed
himself in the history of this community, and the old
testament is, in the first place, the community's attempt
to record and unpack the meaning of that perception. If
we take the historical dimension of our faith seriously we
will want to look into this. Just as we cannot really understand another person without knowing something of his
past, just as we cannot understand man and his place in
the world unless we take account of his evolutionary past,
so we cannot really grasp the meaning of what God did
in Christ without understanding what he was doing in
the community from which Christ came. One of the earliest christian homilies reminds us that he who raised
Jesus from the dead was the god of Abraham, Isaac, and
Jacob (Acts 3:13). In several converging ways the old
testament stands at the heart of our faith.

Coming now to Gen 1–11. Ostensibly it is a history of
the world from creation to the call of God to Abraham
(Gen 12:1–3). While a straightforward first-time reading
might give us many personal insights, it is especially important here to know something of how this 'history'
came to be written. No one supposes nowadays that
Moses wrote the whole of the pentateuch. Apart from the
small difficulty that it contains a circumstantial account
of his own death and burial, there are many indications

that the whole vast complex of history, laws, ritual, reflects a history of literary activity covering some eight hundred years, a history which at the same time mirrors the progressive self-understanding of the community from which the writing came. While there is plenty of room for scholarly debate at practically every point, we may outline the process by which this 'history' came to be written as follows.

Israel began to exist as a community after the various tribes settled in the land of Canaan. They themselves traced their origin back to a great liberating act of Yahweh their God in Egypt where they had been slaves. This conviction finds vivid expression in the passover *haggada* or recital (see Ex 12 and Deut 6:20–25). But the canonical, fixed point of exodus could hardly have been an absolute beginning. Just as, say, an American who wants to understand his history will go back beyond the Declaration of Independence in 1776 to the pilgrim fathers and the history of the thirteen colonies, so Israelite memory went back beyond Egypt to the great migrations which brought their first ancestors into Canaan. Making due allowance for polemical re-editing of ancient material, touching up, legend, and even mythical elements, the stories of the patriarchs are historical, or at least the stuff of which history is made. Archaeologists have no difficulty in situating the patriarchal cycles of stories in the middle bronze age (roughly 2100–1500 BC).

About 1000 BC the tribes came together to form a united nation under David. During his reign and that of his son Solomon there came into existence for the first time the conditions necessary for full-scale historical writing. It was probably at the court of Solomon that a Judaean writer put together the first great national epic of Israel from the creation to the time of writing. It is not quite the kind of history written today: the writer used all kinds of material including myths, he had his own angle on his work, his own points to make, his own axes to grind. In particular, we have to remember that it was a national and royal (or, if you like, messianic) epic. Much later, during or after the exile in Babylon, groups of scholars and priests re-edited the whole of the national history—including the Judaean epic narrative—as part of the preparation for a new Jewish state-church. Here the situation of the editors and their points of view were widely different from those of the epic writer of some four hundred years previously and these differences stand out quite clearly in the final work as we shall see.

Gen 1–11 is a sketch of universal history preparatory to salvation history. It is meant to show the kind of world from which Israel came and into which the saving intervention of God was inserted. By implication, it attempts to explain why salvation was (and is) necessary. On the literary level, as we have seen, it is made up of the first part of the epic narrator's history re-edited and amplified by priests and scholars. We may distinguish their contributions roughly as follows:

GENESIS TEXT	EPIC NARRATOR	PRIEST NARRATOR
1:1–2:4		Creation recital
2:4–3:24	Temptation and fall	
4:1–16	Cain and Abel	
4:17–26	Descendants of Cain and Seth	
5:1–32		Adam to Noah
6:1–4	Sons of God and daughters of men	

GENESIS TEXT	EPIC NARRATOR	PRIEST NARRATOR
6:5–9:17[1]	The flood	The flood (second edition)
9:18–29[1]	Noah and his sons	
10:1–32	The world after Noah	Noah and his descendants
11:1–9	The tower of Babel	
11:10–32		Noah to Abraham
12:1–3	God's call to Abraham	

This bare outline should be referred back to in the course of our study.

Book list

Those who have the time and inclination to go deeper into the study of these chapters could use the commentary of Gerhard von Rad, *Genesis*, London 1961 (Eng trans), which contains valuable insights, and/or that of S. H. Hooke in *Peake's Commentary on the Bible* London 1963, 175–86, set out more fully in the *Clarendon Bible Series, In The Beginning*, London 1947. One should note, however, that Professor Hooke often uses a 'myth and ritual' explanation which not all accept as valid. A briefer and more popular exposition can be found in my *From Adam to Abraham*, London 1965.

Dietrich Bonhoeffer's *Creation and Fall*, London 1959, provides, as we might expect, a remarkably deep and original interpretation of some of the issues behind the first three chapters of Genesis.

[1] Here the two accounts have been conflated so that there is no clear-cut distinction.

Those who wish to read further in the mythological heritage of the ancient near east which we have shown to have so much importance for the interpretation of these chapters will find relevant texts in D. Winton Thomas (ed) *Documents from Old Testament Times*, London 1958. The Penguin edition of the *The Epic of Gilgamesh* is well worth reading in its own right. Also H. Frankfort and others, *Before Philosophy*, London 1949, for a general introduction to ancient mythical thinking.

1

Creation recital
Gen 1:1–2:4

A first reading reveals a clear pattern; it looks, in fact,
very much like a hymn in seven stanzas. The seven days
clearly refer to the Jewish liturgical week culminating
in the sabbath. The priest-writer was naturally much
concerned with worship: the heavenly bodies which
played an important part in determining liturgical oc-
casions (1:14) and the sabbath which was so important
that even God observed it (2:2). Read it carefully and
you will see that the first day (light) corresponds to the
fourth (sun, moon, and stars), the second (firmament
and waters) to the fifth (birds and fish), the third (dry
land and vegetation) to the sixth (animals and man).
This last, incidentally, reflects priestly interest in food
laws which play such an important part in judaism. The
order is artistic not chronological and culminates in the
creation of man announced in solemn tones:

> God created man in his own image
> In the image of God he created him
> Male and female he created them [1:27]

Let us, to begin with, get rid of the idea that we have
here a kind of photographic reproduction of an event
which took place at a definite point in the past as first in
a series. For one thing, as God reminded Job (38:4–7),

9

there was no one around to witness such an event. Is it then a myth? Most ancient peoples had creation-stories some of which were grossly mythological, as, for example, those representing the world originating from the copulation of divine beings. Here creation comes about solely through the creative word of God. Primitive men could not bear to think of themselves as living in an unending time-sequence; they had to have a definite beginning and end to impose some sense and order on the world in which they lived. That is why nearly all of them speak of creation as imposing order on chaos, which is true of this creation account though it does not exhaust its meaning. It at least shows us that creation is concerned much more with saying something about our life in the world here and now than with a past event.

In one of his essays Ian Ramsey, now Bishop of Durham, has an interesting approach to the creation story. The writer, he says, is trying to get us to share his way of looking at the world rather than commit ourselves to certain propositions about how the world began. Imagine the world as one chaotic mass of water; then think of a first stage of order being introduced by the separation of water from dry land; then vegetation, then higher forms of life, and then—man. Here we move from the inorganic to the organic, from the impersonal to the personal and the interpersonal. Along this line God's relationship to the world becomes closer with every stage—'let *us* make man in our image, after our likeness'. The line is continued with the covenant of friendship into which he drew his people, and we are part of that people.

Another point is worth considering. If the creation narrative is more about our life in the world here and now than about a primordial event, what is it trying to say? Here people generally think of dependence and creatureliness, but maybe we shall conclude after a careful reading that there is little reference to this in the narrative. Notice how the sun, moon, stars, and animals, all of which were in one way or another worshipped by surrounding peoples at the time of writing, are denoted and given a severely practical function with regard to man. This is part of what Max Weber calls the disenchantment of nature, man being set free from servitude to divine powers. The world is emptied of useless gods and man's stature grows accordingly. Man is set the task —in Teilhard de Chardin's well-known phrase—of building the world: 'be fruitful and multiply, fill the earth and subdue it' (1:28). But this task can only be performed by free men. Isn't it likely that the reference to man made in the divine image means just this?

A final point. It may seem surprising, but creation is not really a central 'doctrine' in the old testament. God is not named as a creator in any of the oldest divine titles used by the Hebrews. These show that he was associated not with the world or any particular place, as was common elsewhere, but with specific social groups. In particular, he is the god of Abraham, Isaac and Jacob. The covenant-god is, in the first place, he who created a people, who performed the miracle of transforming a slave-gang into a genuine human community which was to be the nucleus of a universal community. Naturally, however, a problem arose for the Hebrews when they settled in Canaan which was familiar with creation-myths and whose chief god, El, was a creator-god. From then on we find them struggling with their idea of god, trying to adapt their thinking to new insights. With the exile there was a real death of god for Israel. In response to a new, much wider and more open situation, prophetic thinking transformed the old national god of Israel, whom we must admit had a rather vicious and narrow-minded streak, into a universal god, a creator-god. His relation to Israel had to be seen in the context of his relation to the world and all the nations. This problem of the relation of Israel to the world is the basic problem in the first eleven chapters of Genesis. For us today it is bound to raise questions about the relation between church and world which modern life also forces on us with increasing urgency.

Further reading in the old testament

Is 43 : 1–13, from the exile period. God creates and gives a mission to Israel.

Job 38, a dialogue about creation.

Ps 104, a creation-hymn based on an Egyptian model.

Ps 136, an antiphonal psalm praising God in creation and history.

One could conclude by reading Is 43 : 1–7 followed by Eph 1 : 4–12.

1. Is this chapter relevant at all to modern cosmological thinking, for example, the 'big bang' and 'continuous creation' theories?

2. How is it possible to reconcile dependence on God, expressed in calling him our creator, and the task of achieving the freedom necessary for 'building the earth'?

3. What light does the biblical doctrine of creation throw on the relation between church and world?

4. For centuries the churches interpreted this chapter literally. Have we christians yet come to terms with language, including biblical language, as symbolic, that is, pointing to rather than containing and defining reality exhaustively? What beliefs tell for and against literalism?

2

Temptation and fall
Gen 2:4–3:24

Preliminary notes

As a glance at the scheme on pp 6–7 will show, this is
the first chapter in the epic narrative, put together very
probably during the reign of Solomon, in any case not
much later. As is natural, it will reflect in different ways
the problems and issues which were live at that time
in Israel, a fact which is not always taken into account
by interpreters. We shall look into this a little later in
this chapter.

Though for convenience we have put Cain and Abel
in a separate chapter we must on no account divide off
what happened outside the garden from the story of
what happened inside it. The importance of this remark
will be seen in the next chapter.

This story seems to presuppose a complete suspension
of the critical faculty. The geography is completely hay-
wire, we have snakes that talk and women made out of
ribs, the man is told to guard the garden but there is no
one to guard it against, just as Cain says that anyone
who finds him will kill him though there is no one
around except his father and mother. This is a re-
minder, in case we need one, that the idiom of communication is different from what we are used to today.
It would be a crude error to suppose that we have here

a naïve and artless story; the picture language is used with the greatest subtlety and depth to present problems which are still only too real. One characteristic of the narrative, and of Hebrew thinking in general, ought to be stressed. The Hebrews generally tried to solve problems, even relatively unimportant problems, historically, by looking for an explanation in the past. So in this section we find attempts to answer questions such as: why do snakes crawl along the ground instead of walking on legs like any other self-respecting animal? Why do women have to suffer when they have children? Why does the human body after death turn into a handful of dust? The answers given do not commit us, and did not necessarily commit the writer, to a definite historical explanation, as if snakes had walked on legs before the curse pronounced on them in 3:14. At a deeper level they insert different kinds of observable phenomena into a world of meaning penetrated by the all-present will of God. The Hebrews had a tremendously strong sense of the unity of the world.

A first reading

In this first section of his work the epic narrator consciously uses pictorial and mythical language though his way of thinking is as far removed from the mythical as could be. If we are to take his meaning we have to make the attempt to understand and penetrate the language in which it comes to us. There is no other way. In keeping with this, we should first read through the narrative in order to identify the principal elements in the author's use of language and then, at a second reading, try to come to terms with the meaning within the myth. This is the method suggested here.

(i) 2:4–14 *The scenario*

Note that the setting here is quite different from that of the priest narrator in the previous chapter. The latter deals with a watery world and the transition from chaos to cosmos, here the setting is the arid desert or steppe-land and the transition from the desert to the sown land. It is not really a creation-story since the world is there already and taken for granted. There is a source of water but no one to put it to use. The cultural background of this story is clearly Mesopotamia where civilisation was built on irrigation. Both the Sumerians and the Baby-lonians had their own paradise-myth which has some-thing in common with the Genesis-myth. Another form of the myth can be found in Ezek 28:11–19 which speaks of the king of Tyre 'in Eden, the garden of God' which was protected by a guardian cherub as in the Genesis story (3:24). He too was created innocent, 'full of wisdom, perfect in beauty', but fell from this high condition and in consequence was cast out of the gar-den. The tree of life is also part of the stock-in-trade of ancient semitic mythology, and the idea of the cosmos surrounded by four great rivers corresponds to an ancient way of thinking (four being the cosmic number). The setting is therefore clearly and consciously mythological.

One point which is often overlooked ought to be made before going any further. Nowhere in the paradise and fall story is the protagonist given a personal name. He is simply the man and his partner the woman. She is given the name Hawwah (Eve) only after the condemnation (3:20) and the man becomes Adam (*Adam* means 'man' or 'mankind' in Hebrew) only at the birth of Seth (4:25). The significance of this for the interpretation of the narrative will be obvious.

(ii) 2:15–17. *The command*

The man is put in the garden and given only the command—not to eat of the tree of the knowledge of good
and evil. If we look at other occurrences in the old testament of the phrase 'to know good and evil' (eg 2 Sam
14:17) we shall see that it has nothing to do directly with
moral discernment; it means to know everything. Since
for the Hebrew knowledge is never purely speculative,
to know here really means *to control;* what is forbidden
is, basically, to seek autonomy, to find the principle and
source of one's being in oneself. Recall that for the
Hebrew God's command, his word, is uttered within
the covenant relationship. It was accepted not as an imposition but a gift, not as a limiting factor but the
essential precondition for a meaningful life. To question
this word is to cease trusting God and therefore, impli-
citly, to break the covenant relationship.

(iii) 2:18–25. *The creation of the woman*

Note, to begin with, that the priest-narrator's creation-
story does not differentiate between the sexes when it
speaks of the creation of man: both male and female
are 'Adam' (1:27)! This again indicates that the writer's
interest is not so much in the origins of sexual differentiation as in explaining something about the relation
between the sexes and in particular their mutual at-
traction. The naming of the animals expresses at the
same time man's kinship with the animal world (we
now have good scientific grounds for asserting this) and
his uniqueness in the order of nature. Only woman is
'a helper fit for him'—and not just fit to bear children,
as Augustine said! The strange surgical operation seems
to have two purposes: to explain the physiological difference between the sexes and the dependence of woman

on man both sexually and socially. To what extent this latter is still valid in the socially much more evolved society of today is of course an open question.

(iv) 3:1–13. *The man, the woman and the snake*

For the Hebrews at the time of writing the snake was an ambivalent symbol. It stood for healing, often by sorcery, and for secret knowledge which gave power and control. That we often find it at the side of or twisted round the naked fertility goddess perhaps provides a clue to its introduction here since 'naked' and 'subtle' represent the same word in Hebrew. We may take it to stand for the orgiastic religion of Canaan in which nudity and sexual promiscuity played such a large part and which exercised such a fatal fascination on the Hebrews, who had only recently graduated from a semi-nomadic state. The writer, however, wants us to concentrate not on what the snake is but on what it says. Beginning with the first loaded question we have a conversation which reveals a great deal of psychological perception. The temptation strikes at the heart of the first couple's faith-relationship with God; it leads them to misinterpret the command as an unwarranted limitation of their autonomy and therefore to distrust God. In the scriptures this is the temptation *par excellence* —even for Jesus himself.

One obvious difficulty. In this account the temptation comes from *within* nature since the snake is one of the animals 'that the Lord God had made'. Both Jewish and christian tradition (eg Wis 2:24), however, connect the fall with Satan who, together with other rebel angels, had 'fallen' before man comes on the scene. Yet this idea of an angelic fall from grace seems to be based on ancient Canaanite mythology (a pretty direct echo of which can be found in Is 14:12). Is there anything more than mythology here?

The sequel shows that stepping outside of the divine command, that is, outside of the covenant-relationship, did not have the effect predicted by the snake. Deep division within the psyche—betrayed in the form of shame at nakedness—is succeeded by division within this first social unit, to be followed by murder and a widening arc of disruption and violence. The rest of the story down to Abraham has the purpose of illustrating this by a series of well-chosen examples.

(v) 3:14–24. *Condemnation and expulsion*

The sentences pronounced by God in inverse order to the interrogation correspond to the condition of existence as we experience it, not to something added. Only the serpent is cursed—God never curses man in the scriptures. 3:15, sometimes called the *protoevangelium* (gospel before the gospel) in the Roman catholic tradition, appears to predict nothing more than a state of mutual enmity between snakes and human beings. It is one of several attempts in these chapters to explain something in terms of origins—in this case the revulsion often felt for snakes. If we are to speak of anything here as messianic it would seem better to refer to the second naming of the woman as the mother of the living (3:20). Here is an implicit affirmation, as death draws in from every side, that the future lies open, that the promise hidden in creation will be fulfilled in spite of the dark reality of sin. This promise is renewed to Abraham (12:1–3) with whom the ebb-tide turns to flow. The moving story of the sacrifice of Isaac (Gen 22) gives us another example of life snatched from the jaws of death.

A second reading

Even a first reading of this section will have raised all
sorts of problems for the christian today who wants to
go beyond a routine assent to church doctrine. Was
there ever a paradisal state of man when he was endowed
with 'preternatural gifts'? Is the author speaking here
'of man's *first* disobedience' or is he rather trying to
spell out something about the human condition as we
experience it? Is the church committed to the view
that a first man, named Adam, committed a sin which
was then transmitted genetically like a disease to all of
his descendants?

All we can do here is to present some exegetical con-
siderations which have to be taken into account in our
discussion. We saw that this first part of the epic narrative (called by scholars the Yahwist document since in
it the divine title is generally 'Yahweh') was put together
at the time of Solomon or shortly after, and will therefore reflect issues and problems which were live at that
time. Anyone who wants confirmation of this, and who
has the time, should read the history of the succession
to David's throne (2 Sam 9–1 Kgs 2, omitting the 'ap-
pendices' in 2 Sam 21–24). This purely secular and
brutally candid narrative is closely related thematically
to the epic narrative. Its main theme is disobedience
expressed in a sexual form which results in death—
David's adultery leading to the death of the child, Amnon's rape of Tamar leading to his death at the hands
of Absalom, Absalom's rebellion expressed by appropriating his father's harem which leads to his death, and
so on. There is also a double fratricide similar to that
of Cain. The picture is a sombre one throughout, but
there is a ray of hope. The son of David and Bathsheba

dies but God gives them another son in his place just as
Seth is given the woman in Gen 4 : 25 'instead of Abel'.
The point is that in spite of the recurring pattern of
disobedience, disorder, and death the divine promise,
implicit in creation and now concentrated in the dy-
nasty, will not be made void. This explains why *the
whole sense* of the Genesis story is messianic rather than
any one verse.

On the most immediate level of meaning, therefore,
the story deals with the crisis in Israel's history constituted by passing from a sacred to an ostensibly secular
way of life introduced by the monarchy. In this sense,
Adam is the king. You recall that Solomon's fall from
grace began with his taking many foreign wives who
'turned away his heart' (1 Kgs 11 : 3). The writer wasn't
worried about him taking many wives; the trouble was
that this implied accepting the foreign gods they worshipped and therefore led to covenant infidelity. Further, if we are to speak of a doctrine of original sin in
the old testament we must attach it to the monarchy.
This is clear both in the prophets and in the Deutero-
nomist school. Hosea says to his countrymen: 'from the
days of Gibeah you have sinned, O Israel' (10 : 9).
Gibeah was the city of Saul, Israel's first king.

The Genesis story is not, however, just for kings. It
contains a warning for Israel as a whole to resist those
elements in their environment which pulled them away
from a unique covenant-relationship with God. In this
sense the garden is the land of Canaan which they held
in trust from Yahweh. It belonged to him. The snake
represents the accommodating religion of Canaan which,
while holding out promises of quick returns, made few
moral demands. The tragedy of the man is the tragedy
of Israel which succumbed to the ever-present tempta-

tion to distrust and doubt the word of their God. Perhaps there is also here, for Israel as for the king, a veiled warning against the danger of marriage with foreign women. But basically the temptation is to what in the scriptures is the greatest sin of all, distrust of God's covenanted word.

Finally, this situation is universalised and given paradigmatical value. This is clear both from the context in which the story is placed, that of a universal history, and the symbolic names—the man, the woman. It should be obvious that the writer had no more access than we have to what happened at the beginning of human history. 'Adam' represents the totality of mankind just as 'Israel' (='Jacob', see Gen 32:28) represents the totality of Israelites. What, then, of a sin passed on genetically from one generation to the next? The element of continuity is certainly stressed in the old testament, but we can no more prove that all humanity is descended genetically from 'Adam' than that all Israelites were descended from Jacob—they certainly were not. In the old testament, genealogy denotes *solidarity* rather than genetic continuity; but solidarity is asserted even more in the category of blessing and curse than in that of genealogy—see, for example, Gen 3:14–19; 4:11 (referring to the Kenite tribe, as we shall see); 9:25 (referring to the Canaanites). It is, moreover, a curious fact that the 'Adam story', of such overwhelming importance for us, is never again referred to in the old testament. Later Jewish tradition—together with many church fathers—tends rather to think of the marriage of sons of God with daughters of men (Gen 6:1–4) as an origins story and speaks much more of what Aldous Huxley calls man's original virtue than of his original sin. In short, we should think more in terms of a paradigm than an origins story, more of solidarity than genetic continuity.

We need not regret having no time to go into the question of evolution since that has moved out of the stage of acrimonious debate (of the Wilberforce *v* Huxley kind, with the suggestion, made by a third party, that he would rather be descended from an ape than from a bishop!) and has really nothing directly to do with Genesis. The unity of the human race can be established without the help of scripture, and the arguments —from gradations of colour groups, distribution of blood groups, interfecundity, universality of psychic characteristics—are well known. The question of human solidarity is, however, a tremendously important issue and one which is central in these chapters and throughout the scriptures. That the condition of fallenness is described in these chapters in terms of division, disruption of human relations, and violence already suggests the final aim of the saving intervention of God which begins with the call to Abraham.

Further reading in the old testament

2 Sam 9–20 and 1 Kgs 1–2, disobedience, sexual sin, and death in David's family.

Ezek 28 : 11–19, the king in the garden of Eden— history mythologised. One could conclude with Rom 5 : 6–21, redemption from fallenness, and Phil 2 : 5–11, Christ contrasted with Adam.

1. How would you set out to argue for the existence of a 'Golden Age' at the beginning of history?

2. Or for belief in tempting agents such as Satan in this modern age?

3. What psychological and religious correspondence is there between the Genesis account of temptation and our own experience?

4. Is there anything against explaining 'original sin' by reference to man's evolutionary prehistory, especially to the existence of violence in sub-human animal groups? (Konrad Lorenz maintains that the rat and man are the only animals which kill intraspecifically!)

5. What are the points of agreement and difference between 'fallenness' and 'alienation' in the marxist sense?

6. Could one still hold that Jesus is the redeemer of all men (Rom 5:12) if Adam wasn't the cause of their sinfulness?

3

Cain and Abel
Gen 4:1–16

Let us repeat, right at the start of this section, that we must carry the story over from the previous chapter even though, as we shall see, there is no question of a real genealogical and chronological connection. After the sin committed in the garden children are begotten *outside* it, and for the writer the kind of children who are born has clearly something to do with what happened inside the garden. In the same way, there is a connection in the mind of the davidic chronicler between the kind of marriage which David contracted with Bathsheba and the death of the child, together with the fratricidal strife which followed. The main theme is banishment. The man and the woman are banished from the garden, Cain is banished from the arable land (in Hebrew called *adamah*) into the wide world; with the flood the descendants of Cain are, so to speak, banished right out of the world. This is a seminal theme throughout the old testament. Read, for example, the story of the banishment of David (1 Sam 26:19) and that of Absalom, the latter brilliantly fictionalised by the wise woman of Tekoa (2 Sam 14) as well as the many passages which speak of the banishment of Israel into exile. In a very real sense, redemption is the opposite of banishment; at the exodus the Israelites are redeemed into a community, a new system of communications. This might prompt some re-orientation of our understanding of baptism. At the popular level, the element which has been most stressed is the *negative* one of exorcism—related directly to a one-sided interpretation of the 'Adam and Eve' story. But what is decisive is surely the *positive* fact that the adult or child is franchised into the community, is redeemed inchoately and in principle from isolation. Does this come through in our various baptismal liturgies?

Coming back to Genesis, let us note how the Cain and Abel story is related to the previous episode. It follows the same pattern: the sin, interrogation, an excuse ('am I my brother's keeper?'), a further curse on the earth (not directly on Cain), expulsion from the *adamah*. This implies that the basic paradigm is repeated but on a wider social scale. But of course there is no literally genealogical link. There is already a developed agrarian society with the institution of sacrificial rites and the tribal blood feud presupposed. Cain fears that whoever finds him will kill him (4:14); a little later we find him building a city (4:17) and his immediate descendants use copper and iron, though the iron age in the near east only starts about 1200 BC, much too late even for Archbishop Usher who calculated the date of creation as 4004 BC! This is one more indication of the fact that continuity is theological, not historical. Estrangement from God resulting from a failure of trust issues in estrangement and disruption within society spreading out in an ever-widening arc which finally engulfs and destroys the whole of society. This illustrates what has been hinted at earlier on, that salvation or redemption (whatever interpretation we give these terms) must be concerned simultaneously with division within the self

—manifested as shame and guilt—and within society —manifested in the form of violence and disruption. Hence the urgency of the christian task of reconciliation and the healing of division in a world threatened as ours is with nuclear extinction.

Coming back once more to Genesis, let us have a closer look at the situation and how it develops. Eve has two children whom she calls Cain and Abel. As is common in the old testament, the former is given a name based on a popular etymology (cf that of Moses in Ex 2 : 10), but in reality the name corresponds to our English name Smith. More of this in the next chapter. The two sons represent two ways of life very familiar to the early Hebrews: the semi-nomadic shepherd and goatherd and the farmer who works the soil. Both offer their sacrifices but Cain's is rejected in favour of Abel's. How did Cain know that God did not accept his offering? We are not told, but he may have deduced it from the fact that his land proved infertile. In 2 Sam 21:1–14 David traces the three-year famine to a treaty-violation committed by his predecessor Saul and attempts to remedy the situation by condoning a ritual murder. Some commentators have interpreted the murder of Abel in the same way, noting that the act is carried out 'in the field' and that the blood flows into the ground. What is important, at any rate, is the banishment of Cain, the fact that he no longer has any settled place in society. Note how, for the writer, to be banished is equivalent to being hidden from God's face (4 : 14) and sent away from his presence (4 : 16); a good example of the intimate correlation in the scriptures between one's personal relationship to God and position in society. Cain is condemned to be 'a fugitive and a wanderer' and ends in Nod, probably a fictional place-name since in Hebrew it means 'wandering'.

Contrary to the view of some apologists for racial inequality, the 'mark of Cain' does not (needless to say) refer to the colour of his skin. We may surmise that it was a tattoo of some kind, but we can no longer recover the meaning it had for the writer. Both here and in the previous chapter God does not leave the sinner to himself. He stays with him. But the line of his promise will continue not through Cain and his descendants but through Seth who is given in place of the dead Abel (4:25).

Further reading in the old testament

2 Sam 14:1–24, the woman of Tekoa's 'fictionalised' account of the banishment of Absalom.

1. To what extent have we underplayed the social dimension of sin and redemption?

2. What light does this section, and the old testament witness as a whole, throw on violence and indicate, even indirectly, what a christian attitude to it entails?

4

Kenites and the development of civilisation
Gen 4:17–26

There is, clearly, some ambiguity in the way Cain is presented. In the first part of the chapter he is a farmer
before being forced to revert to a nomadic life. Here he
is the builder of a 'city' and his descendants embark on
projects connected with what we might loosely call civilisation. As elsewhere in the old testament, the editing
is extremely off-hand. Traditions have been taken from
different sources and given a new meaning in a new
context. The editor has not been too much concerned
to paper over the cracks or smooth out inconsistencies.
Despite these defects, however, he has succeeded in giving us an amazingly coherent picture made up of the
most disparate elements.

In this section Cain is the ancestor and representative
of the Kenite clan (the two names are identical in
Hebrew). The Kenites were a more or less nomadic
group that had wandered for centuries in the area referred to in the old testament as Midian, on either side
of the Gulf of Aqaba. Some of them had penetrated into
the south of Canaan, mixed with the tribe of Judah,
and established settlements or 'cities' there (Kenite
'cities' are referred to in the David story, 1 Sam 30:29).
Kenites and their ancestor Cain are mentioned in the
oracles of Balaam where the seer predicts that 'Cain

shall be wasted'—referring, of course, to the fate of the group (Num 24:21).

It would have been easy for the epic narrator, who came from Judah, to have access to Kenite traditions. According to biblical tradition (Jgs 4:11), Moses' father-in-law was a Kenite and the worship of Yahweh may have come to the Israelites from the Kenites. Once they entered Canaan they came into close relation with the clan of Judah. We can have some idea, therefore, of the interest which the epic narrator's first audience would have shown in Cain and his fate. We have to bear in mind that none of the characters we meet with in these chapters really exists in his own right: Adam, Cain, Lamech, Noah, Shem, Ham, Japheth, even Abraham— these all recapitulate in their persons the characteristics, history, and destiny of groups. This idea of 'corporate personality' may be somewhat inaccessible to us, but has to be borne in mind in our scripture reading. It is of decisive importance for understanding the mission of Jesus as presented in the gospels and by new testament writers in general.

Before reading this potted history of the Kenites we should note that it is wedged in between the birth of Cain and that of Seth (4:1 and 25). The writer wishes to set side by side and contrast two races, the Kenites and the Sethites. Cain was the firstborn, but here as elsewhere in the old testament the younger son is chosen by God in preference to his brother. This is an indirect way of asserting a theological idea of great importance throughout the scriptures. Primogeniture is (or was) a social institution of decisive significance. It embodied and sanctioned the immemorial wisdom by which a particular society preserved and perpetuated itself. The choice of the younger son (Abel, Jacob, Saul, David, etc) is eccentric enough to constitute a sign of a new principle at work. Throughout the old testament this principle, which we can call 'charismatic', continually challenges the forces that make for institutionalisation. This explains, for example, why David had so much trouble setting up an hereditary (as opposed to charismatic) monarchy and why the prophets attacked the institutionalised, hereditary priesthood. For the moment, therefore, the future hope is concentrated on the line of Seth. It is not surprising that many church writers saw this group as a type of the christian church, the new race of mankind.

In reading 4:17-24 we should bear in mind that we have here only a few twisted remnants of very old Kenite traditions and sagas; just as much has survived as suited the epic narrator's purpose. We shall look into the lists of names in the next chapter. A city called Enoch is unknown to history or archaeology and looks somewhat improbable. Among the Kenites the writer singles out for mention three classes of itinerants who can still be found wandering in the desert region below the Dead Sea and in the eastern part of the Sinai Peninsula: shepherds, musicians, and traders in copper. In point of fact Midian was rich in copper and there were also rich copper mines in South Arabia where, as we know from inscriptions, Hebrew slave-gangs worked. This was Kenite country.

It will not have escaped the reader that we have moved a long way away from 'the man' peacefully tilling his bit of garden. If we take in the whole of the narrator's 'primitive history' (Gen 2-11) we shall see that he was evidently interested in the origins of culture and civilisation in its various forms. The man is condemned to work the soil to get a precarious living from it (3:23) but Noah is really 'the first tiller of the soil' (9:20) and the founder of viniculture. The Kenites originated not only cattle-rearing (4:20) but also copper-smelting and music (4:21–22). The clothing-industry is traced back to the dawn of history (aprons of fig-leaves and garments of skins) but only as a *faute de mieux*. Urban civilisation begins with the Kenites (4:17), but cities in the true sense of the word depended on the ability to make bricks with bitumen as mortar, a skill first developed by the Babylonians (in reality by the Sumerians before them) as is acknowledged later (11:3). The writer is also fascinated by the more imponderable elements in this process—the increasing complexity of social and political organisation—the political list in chapter 10—and the origins of language (11:7 ff).

This interest can hardly be dissociated from the intellectual renaissance which derived its inspiration from the court of Solomon, heavily indebted as we know it was to Egyptian influence. Our primary source (1 Kgs 4:29–34 in particular) witnesses to the intellectual activity of this milieu in which the king himself shared, and this is further supported by the attribution of much of the 'wisdom literature' to Solomon. The writer was part of this movement, as his work attests, but his attitude to it was by no means uncritical. This is seen in the section we are discussing by the fact that some decisive forward steps towards 'civilisation' were taken by the Kenites. He is perhaps warning us that what we call culture and civilisation are also subject to fallenness and provide the circumstances in which its consequences can be most easily studied. This was no doubt due in part to his experience of the deterioration induced by contact with Canaanite civilisation and the advent of the monarchy; but his solution is neither a flower-power-like opting out nor a pseudo-romantic return to a golden age. The revolution in social relationships and structures is here to stay and will grow . . . 'this is only the beginning of what they will do, and nothing that they propose to do will now be impossible for them' (11:6). The action henceforth is not against but within this movement.

Further reading in the old testament
1 Kgs 3–4, Solomon's wisdom.

1. How can we best express today the old testament concept of 'corporate personality'?

2. What light does the choice of the younger son over the elder throw on the way God is represented as acting throughout the scriptures in general?

3. To what extent is the narrator over-critical with regard to human progress and civilisation?

5

From creation to uncreation
Gen 5:1–32

With this section we take up the priest narrator's history where it left off at the end of the creation recital. The change in style and presentation can easily be felt—much more stereotyped, formulaic, and ecclesiastical, much more interest in numbers and genealogies. The school from which this writer came had a grandiose concept of history as the arena of the divine activity. The whole span of time is divided into phases and is narrated in distinct series of 'generations' (this is still the word for 'history' in modern Hebrew). According to the systematic history of the priests there are ten 'patriarchs' before the flood (5 : 1–32) and ten after (11 : 10–26). The first series represents primitive, universal history, the second the history of the Semites. As regards the first—with which we are concerned here—some connection certainly exists between it and the Kenite genealogy we read about in the previous chapter; at least five of the names are identical. To complicate things a little more, we have at the end of chapter 4 (4 : 25–26) a fragmentary genealogy of Adam to Enosh through Seth. Enosh is described as the first to institute worship of Yahweh, which appears to contradict Ex 3 : 13–15 and 6 : 2–3, according to which Yahweh revealed himself to Israel for the first time in Egypt. But in fact most modern scholars admit that Yahwism was an old, pre-Israelite cult—perhaps of the Kenites—which was taken over and given a revolutionary new meaning by the Israelites of the exodus period.

Since we are not reading the scriptures as antiquarians we need not linger over details, but one thing about this list ought to be said. The Sumerians who lived in the delta of the Euphrates in the fourth and third millennia BC had a list of kings which numbered ten before the great flood and ten after. The similarities between the priest-narrator's lists and these much older ones make it virtually certain that the former are based on the latter. The third has a name corresponding to the Sumerian name, the seventh in both lists is taken up to heaven (the gods) and the tenth in both cases is the hero of the great flood. The evident if partial literary dependence of Gen 1–11 on mythical prototypes—the Babylonian creation recital, the king-lists, and the flood-story in particular—led some scholars of an earlier age to the hasty conclusion that this first part of the old testament was just a rehash of ancient mythological themes. Nothing could be further from the truth. Here as elsewhere in the scriptures myth is used as the only available thought-category to express and unpack an experience which is (dare we say it?) existential and historical. In much the same way new testament writers use a language which we can describe as mythical even if they themselves would not have used that adjective; but the starting-point is real and in the order of experience—'that which we have heard, which we have seen with our eyes, which we have looked upon and touched with our hands . . .' (1 Jn 1 : 1). In the old testament, the starting-point is the experience of liberation mediated directly to the first Israelites, indirectly and vicariously (through tradition, especially liturgical tradition) to those who came after. The authors we are dealing with here stood directly within that tradition. Liberated from the closed world of myth, they felt free to restate that experience in the only kind of religious language then available. But it would be a mistake to characterise this in a straightforward way as myth.

A very important case of this ambiguity can be studied in this chapter, namely, the way in which the relationship of humanity to God is described. Adam is created 'in the likeness of God' (5:1; cf 1:26–27). In some ancient mythological texts we find the same language, and the likeness is thought of as physical—in fact even here we read that Adam begot Seth 'in his own likeness' (5:3). Church writers have tried in different ways to express what this 'divine likeness' in man can mean. Today we might have to find a different way of putting it. Jung, for example, says that for him the human psyche has the same numinous character that traditional theology ascribes to the deity. How can the biblical statement be meaningful for us today? Enoch who is seventh in the list—recall that seven is the sacred number in the scriptures—lived in perfect association with God. Following his own (to us) obscure theory of numbers, the priest narrator expresses this perfection by giving him 365 years, the same number as days in the year. After this 'he was not, for God took him' (5:24); a statement which for us is not only obscure but misleading since it may give us the idea that one can be too good to live in this wicked world. In the old king-list referred to above, however, Enoch's opposite number is taken up to the gods in order to hear secrets not divulged to all men, and in later Jewish tradition Enoch is one of the great sources of prophetic revelation. Beyond this, however, the writer is expressing a conviction that association with God has within it a force and strength which takes one beyond the reach of death;

and we should note that in the old testament in general
the possibility of surviving death is linked not, as so often
in popular christianity, with an imaginary and mythical
world beyond time, but with a certain kind of experience
available here and now (see, for example, Ps 73).

What of the fantastic ages of these great men of yore,
which gave rise to equally fantastic explanations by some
early church writers? Here again the language is clearly
mythological. If we turn to the king-lists of the Sumerians
we find ages that leave those of the biblical 'patriarchs'
well in the shade, ranging as they do from 18,600 to
36,000 years. What we should note is that in both cases
the length of life tends to decrease. The pre-flood figures
are in the 1,000–700 range, those after the flood between
600 and 200, those from Abraham range between 200 and
100, and later still we hear the psalmist complain that
'the years of our life are threescore and ten or, if we are
strong, fourscore years' (Ps 90:10). Here the priest-narrator is saying the same thing as the epic narrator but in
a different and less accessible way. He is saying that the
further we distance ourselves from the creative centre of
our life-with-God the more our vital energies diminish.
This is not just, as it were, a principle of the 'spiritual
life'. The context within which these figures are placed
shows that the writer is speaking of a condition of estrangement within society and at the same time suggesting how it arose and how it may be overcome.

In accordance with his schematic procedure, the priest
narrator goes from Adam to Noah, then narrows down
the line of Noah to Shem, ancestor of the semites, ending
with Abraham, the only ancestor of Shem he is interested
in. Noah, 'he who brings relief', marks a decisive turning-
point, but here there is a break in the narrative.

Further reading in the old testament

Ps 73, the meaning of association with God.

1. How much religious language is mythological?

2. To what extent does the way these chapters speak of God acting make it difficult for us to take their meaning?

3. If our christian faith is based on experience, as is suggested here, what kind of experience is it?

4. With all the political and racial hatred we see around us today doesn't it sound somewhat hollow to talk of man made in the image and to the likeness of God?

6

A race of giants
Gen 6:1–4

This short passage has no obvious connection, either chronological or otherwise, with what goes before. 'Sons of God', 'daughters of men' and the giant Nephilim are introduced without explanation. It looks like an independent and erratic bit of tradition which has been inserted here by the epic narrator for some purpose of his own. Interesting to note that for many of the rabbis and early fathers of the church this, rather than Gen 3, was the original sin story.

An observant reader will find one important connection between this rather odd mythological fragment and the story of what happened in the garden. In the latter, the Lord God expelled the man from the garden 'lest he put forth his hand and take also of the tree of life, and eat, and live for ever' (3:22). In this story he declares that his spirit will not abide in man for ever, for he is flesh (ie perishable). Ancient mythologies often speak of man attempting to achieve immortality, immunity from death. The ancient semitic epic of Gilgamesh, to be discussed in the next chapter, tells of the hero who watches his friend Enkiddu die and in his ensuing bewilderment and grief sets off to find the plant of immortality. After many adventures he does find it but it is snatched from his hand by a snake. While still on his journey he had been warned by the ale-wife Siduri that his search would be fruitless. 'Gilgamesh', she asks, 'where are you wandering? The life you are seeking you will not find. When the gods created mankind they set aside death for mankind and retained life in their own hands'. Though the biblical author does not share the pessimism of the author of Gilgamesh, he affirms even more strongly that man does not find the source of his own existence in himself. Life belongs to God as of right. Once man begins to act as if the source of his being, his ultimate explanation and justification, lay in himself, he is out of true and the inner contradiction which results is worked out in the form of discord and violence in society.

Just as the man's stepping beyond the limit is followed by the first crime against the person, so here the narrative goes on to speak of wickedness, perversion and violence. We have, therefore, the same pattern as in Gen 3–4—a sexual union the nature and consequences of which are revealed in the kind of children who are born from it. We have seen some historical reasons why the role of sex in society would have been thrust on the epic narrator. While he stresses the creative—not just procreative—possibilities of the man–woman relationship he does not neglect to deal with the temptation of absolutising sexual experience. He could afford to do this since his own tradition, and the whole of Jewish tradition after him, presupposes a healthy, positive attitude to sex. In a basically anti-sexual culture like our own the temptation to trivialise sex will be most obvious, in which respect a reading of the old testament can be of great help to us. The epic narrator is, however, more concerned with another aspect of sexual relations. In both the story of the man living with the woman

and this ancient fragmentary myth of titan promiscuity
the sphere of sexual relations is that in which man's
refusal to accept the limitation imposed on him by the
kind of world in which he comes to consciousness is first
worked out. This is put very clearly and characteristically by Dietrich Bonhoeffer in a passage which could
well serve as a basis for further discussion (it can be
found in *Creation and Fall*, London 1959, 79-80):

> This avid passion of man for the other person first
> comes to expression in sexuality. The sexuality of the
> man who has transgressed his limit is the refusal to
> recognize any limit whatever; it is the boundless pas-
> sion to be without a limit. Sexuality is the passionate
> hatred of every limit, it is arbitrariness to the highest
> degree, it is self-will, it is avid, impotent will for unity
> in the divided world. It is avid because it knows of
> man's common humanity from the origins onwards,
> and impotent because together with his limit man has
> finally lost the other person. Sexuality desires the de-
> struction of the other person as creature; it robs him
> of his creatureliness, violates him as well as his limit,
> hates grace. Man's own life is to preserve and propagate
> itself in this destruction of the other person. Man is
> creative in destroying. In sexuality mankind preserves
> itself in its destruction. Unrestrained sexuality, like
> uncreative sexuality, is therefore destruction *par ex-
> cellence*. Thus it is an insane acceleration of the Fall;
> it is self-affirmation to the point of self-destruction.
> Passion and hate, *tob* and *ra* (ie 'good' and 'evil')—
> these are the fruit of the tree of knowledge.

It should be noted that Bonhoeffer is speaking of sexuality in itself, unrestrained, outside the limit which
our life as social beings invites us to accept—especially

the limit of marriage (see Gen 2:24). Once we have understood the meaning of the myth in its new context, we need not worry too much about its original meaning though one or two aspects may be pointed out. In Hebrew 'sons of God' simply means 'divine beings'. The covenant faith excluded in principle belief in intermediate divine beings but many traces of the old polytheism can be found in the poetical literature of Israel as, for example, when the book of Job refers to the 'sons of God' shouting for joy at the creation of the world (38:7). Stories of marriages between divine beings and human women abounded in both classical and semitic antiquity, first of a *genre* of theological science-fiction of which we have examples today in writers like C. S. Lewis and John Wyndham. Typically, the Hebrews mixed 'pure' myth with historical recollection since the giants who were born of these unions probably refer to their not very scientific interest in the ancient populations of Canaan and Transjordania. Those of their predecessors who were not semitic would have been considerably taller than the Hebrews, which may help to account for half-legendary accounts such as that of the giant Og and his bed (see Deut 3:11—the 'bed' was probably a fallen column like those at Stonehenge). In view of this we may have in this passage another veiled warning against 'mixed' marriages—between Hebrew and non-Hebrew— so often denounced in later writings, especially since 'son of God' is also applied in the old testament to the Israelite in his covenant-relationship to God.

The statement of the Lord, which comes surprisingly in the middle instead of at the end of the passage, is a judgement passed on this attempt to grasp immortality which had eluded the first man and woman. Some have

read it as a prediction of the flood to follow within a
hundred and twenty years—a kind of long-range weather
forecast—but it is better understood as a further limitation of the human life-span. This is another parallel
to the judgements passed on the snake, the woman and
the man at the beginning.

Further reading in the old testament

Ps 82, in which we find some mythological language,
the required recognition of God's overlordship of the
world and, correlatively, the need for social concern.

*1. What help can we get from this passage, and Gen
1–11 in general, towards working out a better understanding of the role of sex in society?*

*2. Do these origin-stories provide any kind of basis
for either affirming or denying the 'doctrine' of immortality?*

7

Uncreation: the great flood
Gen 6:5–9:17

To help the reader find his way through the next long
section we may divide it as follows:

(a) Introduction: the decision to destroy the world,
6:5–13
(b) Instructions given to Noah, 6:14—7:5
(c) Description of the flood, 7:6–24
(d) Description of the ebb, 8:1–19
(e) Sequel to the flood: the covenant with Noah,
8:20—9:17

Here as elsewhere in Gen 1–11 we have a conflation of
two accounts widely differing in theological approach,
style, and presentation. We need to take note of this if
we are not going to waste a lot of time asking whether
seven pairs of animals went into the ark or only one
(as in John Huston's ark in the recent film!), whether
the flood lasted forty days or a hundred and fifty, and
the like. The final editor just wasn't bothered about that
kind of thing. For the most part it will not be difficult
to distinguish the two contributions. The 'priestly' style
comes out in the interest in exact chronology and
measurements. Naturally, these are not to be taken
literally—otherwise we should have to suppose a house-
boat not much smaller than St Paul's cathedral. The

concept of God is also very different. In the earlier version he is, as always in the epic narrative, a very human
God. He makes decisions, changes his mind (that is,
'repents') and is always on the scene, even shutting the
door of the ark after Noah and his menagerie go in. The
priest-narrator's God guides history more directly and
explicitly. In this case, he guides Noah to the first of
those great covenants which make the history of God's
dealings with mankind. As the whole history of Israel
is summed up in the Sinai covenant, so universal history
is in this covenant made 'with all flesh that is upon the
earth' (9:17).

Probably these two accounts were based on two similar versions of a much older flood-story current among
the Sumerians and Babylonians and then disseminated
throughout all the ancient near east. This story occupies
the eleventh of the twelve tablets on which the Gilgamesh epic was first written, though it was in fact older
than the framework in which it was presented. As we
saw in the last chapter, the hero sets off on a journey
in search of the secret knowledge which will enable him
to escape death. After many adventures he finds a certain
Utnapishtim 'at the mouth of the two rivers' (the location of the Babylonian paradise) who is the only mortal
to have attained perpetual life with the gods. Utnapishtim tells him the story of the great flood to show him
how he achieved this end and indicates where Gilgamesh may find the plant of life. He does find it but is
foiled at the last moment by a snake.

Even a casual reading of the old Babylonian, or even
older Sumerian version, will show how closely the biblical accounts have stuck to their prototype.[1] Utnapishtim

---

[1] The Mesopotamian and biblical narratives are set out in

is a good man in a wicked world at the time when the
great gods, for purely capricious reasons, decide to
bring on the deluge. He is commanded to build a large
boat and lay in supplies and livestock. The deluge rages
for a week after which the water subsides, mountain
tops appear and the hero sends out successively a dove, a
swallow, and a raven. At the end there is a sacrifice to
the gods and the latter, at length placated, declare
Utnapishtim to be immortal like themselves.

The first and least important reason for going into
this is to save ourselves the trouble of arguing whether
the bible is here describing a 'real event'. As recently
as 1952 an expedition climbed Mount Ararat to look
for the ark and there are still people who use the archaeological finds of Professor Woolley to prove that such a
flood as the biblical writers describe took place in Mesopotamia in the third millennium. In view of the close
parallelism between the biblical and the older material,
taken with the widespread evidence for flood-stories in
antiquity, the most we can say is that the literary evidence taken as a whole could conceivably reflect some
drastic alteration of human environment at the dawn of
history. To speculate further would distract our attention fatally from the meaning which the story has in
this particular context.

Once we have conceded that while the biblical writers
in these chapters may not have been entirely indifferent
to the question of historical origins, they are far more
concerned with the condition of man here and now, we
can go on to study the way in which they have used
older material, including myth. We have seen the

---

parallel in *Peake's Commentary on the Bible*, London, 1963,
184, and my *From Adam to Abraham*, London, 1965, 98–102.

creation-recital, similar in some respects to the one recited in Babylon during the new year festival which
lasted seven days; the paradise-myth widely disseminated
in the ancient near east; the myth of 'divine' marriages.
To these we shall have to add Nimrod the mighty
hunter (10 : 8–9) and the tower of Babel (11 : 1–9). As
we have just seen, the flood-story formed an important
chapter in the epic of Gilgamesh, the basic theme of
which is a journey in search of an answer to death or,
if you wish, of ultimate meaning in a life which is
bounded by death. Some scholars understand the flood
through which Utnapishtim passed as a *rite de passage*,
a ritual which initiated one into a new life. Gilgamesh
is searching for the ritual which will enable him also to
pass through into new life, but this is not given to mankind at large—'the life you are seeking you will not
find'. In their own versions of the flood-story the biblical
writers pass judgement on man's attempt to grasp for
himself a boundless and autonomous existence. How
man is to share in the divine prerogative of life, how he
is to defeat death, is first revealed in the call to Abraham,
who sets out on a journey rather different from that of
Gilgamesh.

We have here inchoately some of the central christian
themes: life as a venture of faith, Christ as the centre
and pattern of the new life ('who, though he was in the
form of God, did not count equality with God a thing
to be grasped'), baptism as a passing over into a new
life (see 1 Pet 3 : 20–21).

One further aspect of the great flood-story which is
often overlooked ought to be noted in our study. The
world which is destroyed is the same world of the great
creation-prologue in the first chapter. The world in
which order first arose out of a primeval watery chaos

is now reduced to the watery chaos out of which it arose—chaos-come-again. The firmament which keeps the great deep at bay is now perforated: 'all the fountains of the great deep burst forth, and the windows of the heavens were opened' (7:11). Underlying this there is, perhaps, the idea that as man removes all limits in an attempt to achieve autonomous existence, God removes the limits placed at the beginning. The world will just not bear this limitless kind of life—it's not that kind of world. Note further how the destruction takes place in much the same order as creation: first, the earth itself is covered as high as the highest mountain, then 'birds, cattle, beasts, all swarming creatures that swarm upon the earth, and every man' (7:21). We can draw two important theological conclusions from this. First, that man's existence in the world is not, so to speak, an absolute datum; it lies between the poles of creation and uncreation, subject to God's providence and judgement. Second, that the destiny of the whole order of creation is tied in with that of man, that henceforth the end of the whole process implicit in creation can be worked out through conscious human activity, the conscious assumption of responsibility by men working in tandem with God. Despite the archaic terms in which it is presented, this view of the world and our existence in it is more relevant than ever in a world threatened with nuclear overkill.

The last section of the story (8:20–9:17) comes from the priest-narrator. It tells of the first act of cult on the purified earth, the blessing of the new humanity, and the covenant with Noah. This looks like a new creation, but the situation is not quite the same as in the beginning, one sign of the difference being that man now kills for food (9:3). We even have the impression that

God has only now realised what man is really like (the imagination of his heart is evil from his youth) and learned to come to terms with that knowledge. The covenant with Noah, that is, with humanity as a whole, is to be followed by that with Abraham (Gen 17) and finally with Moses (Ex 24:7–8; 31:16–17)— a gradually narrowing field of vision which provides the key to understanding the concept of history in this narrative. The sign and pledge of this universal covenant is the rainbow which represents not a weapon of war (and therefore a threat) but the presence of the invisible God (cf Ezek 1:28). There is, perhaps, also a hint that God himself will abjure violence only if men assume responsibility for their brothers. Violence and exploitation had caused the flood (6:11–13); they were to be absent from the new life offered after the flood.

Further reading in the old testament

Ps 14, human folly and violence; divine judgement.

Jer 4:23–26, chaos-come-again, divine judgement as an undoing of creation (all the cities are in ruins).

1. To what extent does Gen 1–11 offer a serious analysis of society in terms of alienation, exploitation, and violence? (NB *the divine judgement of the flood is provoked by violence, 6:11–13*).

2. How does the new testament make use of the flood-story? (*see especially Mt 24:37–38: Lk 17:26–27: 1 Pet 3:20–21*).

3. How can we speak meaningfully today of divine judgement?

8

A new start: the sons of Noah
Gen 9:18–29

After the clean sweep of the flood we enter with Noah and his sons into a new phase of history. Not, of course, that the flood marks the mid-point between the beginning and the call to Abraham in any realistic sense. This should be obvious from the preceding chapter. But there is some correspondence between the theological presentation of history before and after the great flood. 'Adam' is the ancestor and representative of all humanity. Noah of the new humanity which, however, is thought of in a much more political way than before, since the sons of Noah are the ancestors of the nations known to the Hebrews at the time of writing. Corresponding to the 'original sin' of humanity there is now the 'original sin' of Canaan, ancestor of the people who lived in Canaan when the Hebrews entered some time in the thirteenth century BC. This sin also has the object of expressing something characteristic of the Canaanites as seen by the author and the community to which he belonged. Moreover, the sin of Ham (Canaan) breaks up the new political community in the same way as the sin of the man results in social disruption. The same pattern after as before.

A careful reader will notice here the same kind of editorial inconsistencies as we found in the first chapters. The sons of Noah, to take one example, were already married before the flood yet we find them here living with their father in his tent, evidently unmarried. More important, the pronouncements of Noah (9:25–27) envisage only the populations of the land of Canaan whereas the introductory verse and the so-called table of the nations (chapter 10) understand them to be the ancestors of the whole of the new humanity. There is also some doubt as to whether Ham (9:22) or Canaan (9:25) was guilty of the crime here described. Since, however, these difficulties do not in any way affect the message which the writer wants to convey we can, after noting them briefly, pass on with a good conscience.

After giving us the tripartite division of the new humanity (the semitic, hamitic, and indo-european races) the writer goes on at once to describe its first fall from grace, the sin of Ham (Canaan). Here, as elsewhere in the old testament, the punch-line comes at the end— the triple curse on the sinner. This story has some decidedly odd features. Noah is presented as the inventor of the vine, the founder of viniculture. Apparently he sampled this new and beneficial discovery without due regard for the consquences and got drunk—there had to be a first time even here. Venturing into the tent Ham saw his father naked—apparently also for the first time—and went to tell his brothers, who proceeded to take extremely elaborate precautions before covering him up. The curse and blessings follow as soon as Noah came to and found out what had happened.

The very oddness of the story hints at a further meaning which the writer wants us to grasp. Ham is the ancestor of Canaan, and we have abundant evidence both in Canaanite literature and the old testament that the culture and religion of this people were dominated by the sexual. Naturally the old testament, especially the legislation and the denunciation of the prophets, only gives us one side of the picture—unrelieved sexual depravity, orgiastic festivals, cult prostitutes of both sexes (called 'holy ones') and the like. For the Canaanites themselves, being a predominantly agrarian group, fertility was the main concern and the sexual element in their religion was the means of integrating this area of experience into the world of the sacred and, at the same time, promoting the immanent forces of growth and fertility. It was, perhaps, more functional than the old testament gives us to understand, though of course it also gave plenty of scope for what Aldous Huxley called 'downward transcendence'. At any rate, the story clearly has the primary purpose of expressing the horror which the pious Israelite felt at these practices. This comes through not only in the rather exaggerated precautions taken by the two brothers but in the nature of the sin itself which seems to have implied something more than immodesty (the writer speaks of what Noah's youngest son had done to him).

While on this subject, it might still be necessary to note that the writer is not advocating teetotalism. Wine not only gladdens the heart of man (Ps 104:15) but even rejoices the gods (Jgs 9:13). The vineyard first planted by Noah was to become a symbol of the joy of the kingdom. The wine drunk by Jesus before his death, and which he looked forward to drinking new in the kingdom, was to be drunk to the end of time by those united to him and among themselves in fellowship.

To return to Noah and his sons. The function of the story about the sin is, of course, to introduce the pronouncements of Noah. Since Noah's death at an advanced age is referred to immediately afterwards, the writer may have intended to give them added weight by presenting them in the familiar category of 'famous last words' found so frequently in the old testament. It is clear, at any rate, that they are meant to say something about the groups represented by the ancestor, in the same way as the blessings of Jacob in Gen 49 (also 'famous last words') refer not to twelve individuals standing round the deathbed but to the twelve tribes and their later history. The perspective is here not the whole world but the land of Canaan. Canaan (no longer Ham) is the semitic population which the Hebrews found in possession when they arrived on the scene. Shem represents not the semitic races as a whole but the Hebrews only, while Japheth stands for those indo-european groups which, as we now know from non-biblical sources, were in Canaan side by side with the Canaanites before the Israelite settlement. The three-fold curse is a kind of theological rationalisation of the eventual subjection of the Canaanites to the Israelite tribes. If we look at the history, we shall see that this process was only completed shortly before the time of writing, when the kingdom was consolidated under David. It provides one more example of the extraordinary and unique sense of national destiny alive in Israel as early as that time; the conviction that for some reason God had chosen them as the secret centre of history to bring about his purposes in the world.

Further reading in the old testament

Gen 49, the blessings of Jacob on the tribes.

Deut 4:32–40, God's choice of Israel among the nations.

This passage presupposes the essential political *unity of mankind. What part has the church to play today in the process of reunification?*

9
The world of the nations
Gen 10:1–32

In this chapter the perspective takes in not just Canaan but the world of the nations as known to the Israelites at the time of writing. Note that the lists are in inverse order to the names as given in the introductory verse. This places Shem last and thus facilitates the process of narrowing down until we come to Abraham, the first Hebrew.

The lists of peoples derive, for the most part, from the priest-narrator but are clearly based on ancient material. We may reasonably suppose that the solomonic renaissance of which we spoke earlier involved some systematisation and expansion of geographical knowledge, as did the European renaissance of the fifteenth century. Needless to say, these lists are not based on scientific ethnology. Thus, the semitic Canaanites are grouped with the hamitic Egyptians, the Hittites, who are indo-aryan, are grouped with the Canaanites. The groupings are more geographical and political than ethnic. The *Japheth* group, principally indo-european, represents the scattered remnants of what was once the great Hittite empire. The area covered is mostly Asia Minor and the Levant, and the 'nations' include Greeks, Etruscans, Armenians, Cypriots, and even inhabitants of present-day Russia and Spain. The *Hamitic* group takes in the only part of the African continent generally known at that time, including Egypt, the Sudan, Lybia, and Somaliland. The *Semites* (this term was first coined in the eighteenth century) constitute those nations created as a result of successive waves of invaders from the Syrian and Arabian deserts into the fertile crescent. Among them were 'the sons of Eber', known in the cuneiform inscriptions as *habiru,* to which group the biblical Hebrews belonged.

It is surprising in how many different ways these chapters affirm the unity of the human race. In this case the affirmation is on the political level; not only are they all of the same stock, all part of the new humanity beginning with Noah, but they all spoke the same language (11:1) and were in active intercommunication. But the writer was only too aware that this was an ideal picture. The sin of Ham (Canaan) had already introduced once again the seeds of disunity, and the breakdown in international communications was to be complete with the confusion of tongues described in the next chapter. Now one remarkable fact about these lists will emerge if we take the trouble to wade through them; there is no mention of Israel. The reason is not just that the writer is describing the world before Israel entered it. He is looking out at the world from an epicentre around which this great political circle is drawn, which implies that for him Israel is *the secret centre of history.* The reason for this becomes clear when we reach the point to which all this history is moving, when Abraham—representing Israel—receives his mission and the blessing which will flow from him to all the nations of the earth (12:3).

Most christians have noticed by now that the church is no longer at the centre of the political and international scene today, now that christendom has broken up once and for all. What, then, of the church's mission? Has it to be relegated to the personal and private sphere, leaving politics to the politicians? Has the church in England anything more to do than fill in the gaps left by the welfare state? Is it condemned to travel in the slipstream of the really creative processes that are going on in the world, picking up and giving spiritual first aid to those who 'fall by the wayside'? Nobody really knows the answers to these questions as yet, so meanwhile it might help to study how the mission of Israel, implicit in the call to Abraham, was worked out. It took Israel centuries to understand how this mission was to be carried out; only when she had been scattered among the nations did she begin to rid herself of false ideas of power and abjure a god who became all too often a projection of national power and prestige. It would take us beyond our present purpose to follow this up, but we may at least surmise that the absence of Israel from the list of nations reflects this lesson learned the hard way. Does this have anything to say to the christian church today?

A last point. The hamitic subdivision contains a rather strange fragment of ancient tradition about Nimrod a mighty hunter (10:8–12) who founded the great empires of Babylonia and Assyria. Whether the writer was thinking of the Assyrian war-god Ninurta or Gilgamesh the half-legendary hero of the epic, the name certainly represents the empire of the Assyrians, one of the cruellest and most exploitative political powers of antiquity. It appears that this has been inserted here to prepare the reader for the story of the tower of Babel which, in the form of a political satire, attacks the whole structure of power-politics at its root. But we had better leave this to the next chapter.

Further reading in the old testament

Is 42:1–9, the lesson learned in exile: Israel's mission of service.

   1. How can the church contribute to the unity of mankind?

   2. How did Israel's idea of its mission to the world develop throughout its history? What lessons can it have for us?

10
The city and tower of Babel
Gen 11:1–9

The tremendous publicity which the story of the man and the woman and their sin has enjoyed in the churches has had the bad effect of blurring out the rest of the picture presented in these first chapters. The first eleven chapters of Genesis contain a series of original sins: the first and prototypal sin of disobedience, the first murder (4:8), the origin of the blood-feud (4:23–24), the tainted origins of many of the arts and crafts of civilisation (4:20–22), another original sin of pride and titanism (6:1–4), the first drunkenness (9:21), the prototypal unchastity (9:22–24), the first empire-building (11:2–7). The method of procedure throughout is uniform: the author is analysing the ills of society and presenting the results of his analysis to his reader in the form of prototypal and paradigmatic actions.

This should give us a good angle from which to see what lies behind this apparently naive and artless story about the first attempt to build a skyscraper. Some nomads from the east settle in the plain of Shinar and decide to build a city and a very high tower. The city is Babylon (11:9, Babel, similar to Hebrew *balal*, meaning to speak gibberish) and the tower refers to the great ziggurats, the remains of some of which are still standing in the sandy wastes of the lower Euphrates valley.

In keeping with the method used throughout, the writer has used the great city of Babylon and the most imposing product of its civilisation to analyse a further aspect of fallenness in man's life in society. If we take it purely as a story, it will be difficult to see what there was wrong in wanting to build a high tower. For a theological answer we have to look at the motivation: '. . . let us make a name for ourselves before we are scattered abroad'. Here it is a question no longer of an individual but a whole social and political group which introduces a discordant and divisive element into human relations, and this group is one which can be identified in history.

It's clear that the writer has in mind the historical record of Babylon, its civilisation and its empire. The high point of its achievement had been under Hammurapi of the famous code, almost eight hundred years before the time of Solomon. But Babylon was still a great city and was to remain the archetype of the imperialist and colonialist state. It was by the waters of Babylon that the Israelites in exile were to sit down and weep (Ps 137). Poems from the exilic age in the Isaian collection refer to it as 'the glory of kingdoms' (13 : 19), 'day star, son of dawn' (14 : 12), 'mistress of kingdoms' (47 : 5). It was finally conquered by Cyrus in 539 BC but retained its image for centuries, as we can see from the book of Revelation (chapters 17–18).

Read in this light, the story traces the origins of fallenness on the international level to the founding of Babylon, which was for the writer *the* example of the violent and exploitative manipulation of political power. The writer condemns not only the political but also the religious aspect of Babylonian culture, and he does this by speaking of their deciding to build not just a *city* but a *tower*. As we have just seen, the tower refers to the

Babylonian ziggurat. These ziggurats were temples originally representing the primeval mound of creation, the first to appear above the waters of chaos. They were the focus of the religious life of the city (there was no real difference between religion and politics), which implies that the writer is condemning religion as a function of the political establishment and the means of legitimising and authenticating the existing political structures. In much the same way, the great prophets of Israel were to condemn the official religion with its sacrifices and elaborate liturgy as a kind of umbrella under which all sorts of injustice and exploitation could flourish (see, for example, Amos 5:21–24; Is 1:10–17). This may give us occasion to ask whether the christian churches have not sometimes assumed this questionable role.

Interesting and somewhat odd the way in which this grandiose scheme was thwarted. Previously all had spoken the same language, but in order to spike their guns God confused the speech of the builders so that they could not understand each other and gave up the project in despair. This is obviously one of several popular 'origin-stories' found in these chapters; the answer to the kind of question children keep on asking: why do people speak different languages? why can't all those damn foreigners speak English? The real meaning, of course, lies at a deeper level. The writer is using the language-barrier as a symbol of the breakdown of communication among men, and he sees this as a religious problem—no doubt for the first time in history. This points, perhaps more directly than anything else in these chapters, to the nature of that 'salvation' the history of which begins with the call to Abraham through whom blessing was to come on all the nations. In keeping with this, the church's mission is first of all to heal division, to create a new communication-network among men by being a community of love and mutual responsibility. The story of the day of Pentecost in Acts 2 is probably just as much a paradigm as the story of the tower of Babel. In showing us how, for a few minutes, the language-barrier was broken down among men representing all the then-known continents, the writer wishes to express what is the essential mission of the church. We still have that mission today.

Further reading in the old testament

Ps 137, 'By the waters of Babylon . . .'

Is 13:1-22; 14:4-21; 47:1-15; Jer 50:2-46, poems and sayings against Babylon. One could conclude by reading Acts 2:1-13.

1. What light does this story throw on the church's mission to heal disunity?

2. How does it point to the political and social responsibility of the christian in the world today?

11

From Noah to Abraham
Gen 11:10–32

The genealogy containing ten names in this chapter corresponds to the list of ten before the flood (chapter 5).
Each list ends with three sons and gives the ages of each.
The former is the list of men in the first period of world
history, the latter of the semites. While it is evidently arti-
ficial, it would be wrong to think of the priest-narrator
just making it up out of his own head. One curious indication of its antiquity is that at least five of the names are
names of cities or settlements known to us from the archaeology of the middle bronze age, that is, from the beginning of the second millennium before Christ. In particular,
Haran was a flourishing city in the nineteenth and eighteenth centuries. The movement from 'Ur of the Chal-
deans' (11:31) and from Haran to Canaan (12:4) fit in
very well with what we know of race movements at that
time, in particular the great Aramaean migration into
Canaan at the beginning of the second millennium.

This, incidentally, points to something centrally important in the old testament as a whole. The bulk of the
historical narrative contained in the old testament is
made up of the community's interpretation of its own
history in accord with its own peculiar insights. While for
the Greeks it was the world itself, the static cosmos, which
disclosed a mystery the explanation of which lay beyond

the world, for the Hebrews the area of disclosure was history. That is why in the bible (as one scholar put it) it is not what *is* as opposed to what seems to be which is important, but what *happens*. So, for example, the exodus from Egypt was, from the purely historical point of view, one of several exoduses (see Am 9 : 7); but when the biblical authors say God *led* us out of Egypt, rather than simply, we *left* Egypt, they are speaking of this exodus as containing for them a unique disclosure. The same for the journey of Abraham from Haran to Canaan. Historically, it fits in perfectly with what we know of the Aramaean migration westwards at that time; but by speaking of it as caused by God's call to Abraham (12 : 1), they are giving expression to a new meaning which they have discovered in the history. This gives us a good starting-point for discussing the meaning of the term 'revelation'.

With the call of Abraham 'universal' history dovetails into 'sacred' history. But what is the difference? This question is not so easy to answer as may appear. God is represented as active before Abraham, as we have seen. The priest-narrator speaks of a covenant with Noah preceding these with Abraham and Moses which lie within the usual definition of sacred history. Moreover, Abraham himself is part of the 'pagan' world; according to Joshua addressing the tribes at the great meeting held at Shechem, he 'served other gods' (Jos 24 : 2), and we know now that the identification of 'the God of Abraham, Isaac and Jacob' with Yahweh the Israelite God is secondary and unhistorical. 'The God of Abraham, Isaac, and Jacob' in fact stands for several manifestations of deity worshipped by different groups during the age of the patriarchs. We have no reason to believe that Abraham 'changed his religion' when he accepted God's call to set off on a journey. Why, then, should we speak of 'sacred' history beginning at this point?

For an Israelite, the answer would surely have to be sought in the mystery of divine election. God chose Abraham to be the instrument of fulfilling the first stage of his promise, the formation of a people who would live in the land he was to give them. Abraham accepted that call *in faith* by setting off on a journey to an unknown destination. Both elements are emphasised in the narrative before us. Abraham was to be the ancestor of a great nation, yet 'Sarai was barren; she had no child'! (11 : 30). Here we are being prepared for the moving account of the sacrifice of Isaac (Gen 22), which illustrates both the way in which the divine election works and the need for absolute trust in and commitment to God's purpose in our lives.

With Abraham's setting off on a journey into the unknown, history takes a new direction. The promise which accompanied that act of trust and commitment implies that eventually an answer will be given to the question which arises out of the human predicament described in the previous chapters. The predicament is still ours and the question still has to be answered.

Further reading in the old testament

Gen 22, the near-sacrifice of Isaac, election and faith. One could also read Rom 4; Gal 3 : 6–29; Heb 11 : 8–12 on the christian significance of Abraham and his history.

1. What is the meaning of the term 'sacred history'?

2. What does the relation between 'universal history' (Gen 1–11) and 'sacred history' (Gen 12 : 1 ff) tell us about the relation between the world and the church?

3. *Has our reading of these chapters given us any new angles on the question of revelation?*

4. *What is the real biblical meaning of faith?*

Genesis 12–50

Joseph Blenkinsopp

Introduction

Whether a text from the past can speak to us and enlighten us depends almost entirely on the kind of questions we put to it. This short introduction, and for that matter what follows it, is intended simply to help us to ask the right questions.

Why read these old stories?

Some of them, but not all, are certainly entertaining, given a certain degree of insight and appreciation. There is movement, tension, drama, humour, even sex, but why these rather than, say, *The Thousand and One Nights*? If an answer to this question does not emerge in the course of our study and discussion then this section will obviously not have been worth writing. It is no longer possible to appeal to the 'authority' of scripture in the way many christians used to, and in fact continue to; at least, many of us feel that the problem has now to be approached differently. Perhaps the best solution is simply to begin reading these chapters and work out our own answers to this question as we go along. One point, however, could be made at the outset. The history of the patriarchs has penetrated deeply into the collective memory of the judaeo-christian community and is therefore, whether we are conscious of it or not, part of the past out of which we live. Our reading will, therefore,

involve a clarifying of that past and our interpretation
will necessarily also be self-interpretation. Artless as they
may seem at first reading, these stories may come at some
stage to challenge our self-understanding both as individuals and as members of a faithful community.
Whether this ever happens, will, however, depend on
the degree of involvement we bring to the task and, as
just said, on the quality of the questions we ask.

How not to read them

One mistake to be avoided at all costs is that of distilling
out of these stories 'spiritual' or 'moral' lessons—the kind
of homiletic material you find in the bottom section of
The Interpreter's Bible. Just as bad, if not worse, is the
practice of using them as pegs on which to hang insights
or theories of our own. What is much more difficult, because calling for patience, reflection and sensitivity, is to
get at what is going on here, what it is all about. This is
what we want to attempt. We are not going to hang anything on to these stories. What we will aim at is to bring
to clarity what is there. To interpret is, first of all, to
remove obstacles to understanding what is there, to
allow the text to speak, to tell us what it is there for.

How Gen 12–50 came to be written

A brief glance at the Synopsis will tell us, what we probably know already, that these chapters are made up for
the most part of stories or, to use the term first introduced in this context by Hermann Gunkel, *sagas*. These
deal with the fortunes of a tribal group which migrated
from Mesopotamia to Palestine and ended up in Egypt.
The time-span is, ostensibly, four generations (Abra-

ham, Isaac, Jacob, the sons of Jacob), though other chronological indications scattered throughout would indicate a considerably longer period of time. Many if not most of these stories had their own independent existence before being edited into the complex as we have it. Many if not most were traditioned orally before ending up where they are now. By using established critical methods (form-criticism, traditio-historical criticism) and analogy we can, to some extent, get an idea of what they looked like and what their original point was before they were incorporated into the present ensemble. But much remains uncertain, and in some cases we cannot even be sure who the original hero or protagonist was.

In the course of time individual narratives would have been collected into larger units or saga-cycles. The presence of parallel versions of the same event, examples of which will occur frequently in our reading, suggests that a common fund of traditional material has come down to us from Judah and the Northern Kingdom respectively. In some few cases we even have three versions of the same incident, as with the endangering of the ancestress.

By far the most important of the narrative-cycles have to do with Abraham, Isaac and Jacob. Since there is relatively little about the second of these we may consider Isaac as something of a link figure. Although Abraham came to be taken for granted as the father of the Jewish people, a glance at a concordance will show that he is mentioned very much less frequently in pre-exilic writings than Jacob, Israel is named after Jacob, not Abraham, and it is he who is the 'wandering Aramaean' in the ancient form of words which accompanied the offering of the firstfruits (Deut 26: 5–10). This suggests that in some important respects Jacob is a more primordial figure than Abraham. The latter's memory was cherished particularly at Hebron, a Judaean city where David was first crowned, and it is clear that his position in the tradition owes a great deal to the political ascendancy of Judah over the other tribes.

The cycle of narratives about Joseph (chapters 37–50) is of quite a different kind; much more novelistic and probably more fictional. Indirectly it testifies to the outstanding importance of the 'Joseph tribes' (Ephraim and Manasseh). There are indications, not all in Genesis, that narrative-cycles concerning other tribes also existed. What we find in these chapters represents only a small fraction of what there once was.

It will be obvious that this great complex of traditions has been edited from later viewpoint, that of all-Israel, the tribal federation which became a monarchic state. Hence we have to pay attention to the *functional* aspect of stories about the tribal 'heroes' (some of them none too heroic)—their births, exploits and misadventures. These may, for example, reflect the origins, vicissitudes and, in some cases, eclipse of individual tribes. The genealogical link is clearly, in some cases, a device for ordering the material and expressing relationship, relative status and rank of seniority as between different tribal groups. The renaming of Jacob as Israel, to take a final example, gives expression to Israel's consciousness of election, spiritual identity and destiny. These are only some indications of how necessary it is to bring to bear on each passage as we read it an understanding of the overall intentionality which went into the writing. Only in this way will the meaning, what was meant, emerge, and what was meant is the only basis of any possible meaning for us.

Despite the great gap in time and all that has happened in between, there is a certain similarity between the way Israel, at each stage of its history, re-activated the old tradition about the patriarchs, and the way the christian is invited to do so. In Israel historiography (writing about the past) was always in one way or another a form of understanding and coming to terms with the present, an exercise in self-understanding, a confession of faith or an acknowledgement of failure. Progress into the future was possible only at the price of this renewed self-understanding. That past, present and future are indissolubly linked is a truth which was never so much needed as it is today.

History, myth, legend or what?

While a serious reading of any records from the past must always end up with the question of contemporary meaning it cannot neglect to ask whether and to what extent the records are historical. Here, however, there are some traps into which even eminent scholars fall on occasion. A fairly obvious one is a too great reliance on the results of archaeological work which are held to 'prove' (rarely 'disprove') the biblical record. With respect to the patriarchal saga-cycles, all we can say is that they fit quite well into the background of the first half of the second millennium BC in so far as it can now be reconstructed (numerous interesting examples are given in E. A. Speiser's *Genesis* in the *Anchor Bible* series). Much more insidious is the temptation to foist on to the authors or editors of these ancient stories modern ideas of historical 'truth'. To avoid this temptation we must not ask questions like 'did it really happen?' too early—certainly not before we have some idea of the literary form of the passage, which often betrays the intention behind it, the depth of oral tradition behind a narrative, evidence for editorial activity, and similar matters. And even after we have asked these questions we may still have to admit that we just don't know whether what is recorded happened as recorded or not.

Book list

The commentaries of G. von Rad (*Old Testament Library* series) and E. A. Speiser (*The Anchor Bible*) may be suggested. The former is more theological, the latter more historical and technical, but both are of high quality and intended for the educated reader rather than the scholar. A reading of the relevant section of J. Moltmann's *The Theology of Hope* may also be suggested for further penetration into the main theological issue of these chapters, with special reference to the possibility of christian–marxist dialogue. Other incidental readings, such as the first chapter of E. Auerbach, *Mimosis,* and the sermon in John Osborne's *Luther*, have been suggested at different points throughout this small commentary.

It is perhaps unnecessary to urge that the reader should form his own provisional conclusions on the basis of a careful reading and re-reading of the actual text, before appropriating the views of other writers and scholars, no matter how illustrious.

Synopsis

Arranging the cycles of narratives from the birth or emergence to the death of the ancestral 'hero' has the disadvantage of considerable overlap but it seems the only way to do it since each is certainly an important figure in his own right. Some stories, while principally about one ancestor, also involve another. As a general rule these will be listed in both cycles though discussed only in one. This procedure leaves us with only two narratives which are principally concerned with Isaac, indicating, as we have seen, that Isaac survives only as a link-figure between the more prestigious Abraham and Jacob. Isaac in fact has something of a ghostly existence. Many stories must have been in circulation about him but have not survived. Some few may have been transferred from him to either Abraham or Jacob, though this would be difficult to prove. The introduction to the Joseph cycle —'this is the history of the family of Jacob' (37: 2)—indicates that what follows is only an excerpt from a longer series of narratives involving many if not all of the tribal 'heroes'. Some of these feature quite prominently in the cycle, though subordinated to the figure of Joseph.

The Abraham cycle (12:1–25:10)

1. The call and the promise. Journeying through the land (12:1–9)

2. The endangering of the ancestress (12:10–13:1; 20:1–18; 26: 6-11)
3. Separation of Lot and Abraham (13:2–18)
4. The battle of the nine kings, Melchizedek and Abraham (14)
5. Covenant with Abraham (15 and 17)
6. Sarah and Hagar (16)
7. Theophany at Mamre. The fate of Sodom and Gomorrah (18–19)
8. The birth of Isaac and the saving of Ishmael (21)
9. The binding of Isaac (22:1–19)
10. Epilogue. Last disposition of Abraham. His death (22:20–25:10)

The Isaac cycle (21:1–35:29)

1. His birth. The saving of Ishmael (8 above)
2. The binding of Isaac (9 above)
3. Finding a bride for Isaac (24)
4. The birth of Esau and Jacob. The sale of the birth-right (1 below)
5. Isaac and Rebekah in Gerar (2 above)
6. Isaac's dealings with the Philistines (26:12–33)

The Jacob cycle (25:19–50:14)

1. The birth of Esau and Jacob. The sale of the birth-right (25:19–34)
2. Deathbed blessing on Jacob and Esau (27:1–45)
3. Jacob finds Rachel. Theophany at Bethel (27:46–29:14)
4. The sons of Jacob (29:15–30:24)
5. Jacob and Laban (30:25–31:16)
6. Jacob's return. The first stage (31:17–55)

1

The Abraham cycle
Gen 12:1–25:10

1. Gen 12:1–25:10. The call and the promise. Journeying through the land

We must first direct our attention to the link between the theological outline of 'universal history' in Gen 1–11 and the new history which is now beginning. What marks the first is the seeming impossibility for men left to themselves of creating genuine community. The history begins with banishment and ends with the scattering of the nations over the face of the earth (11:9). With the call and command to Abraham a new initiative begins, blessing takes the place of curse, the ebb turns to flow. Note that there is no mention of the 'conversion' of Abraham. We are told elsewhere that he and his group 'served other gods' (Josh 24:2) and the mention of Yahweh is naturally a retrojection from a later age (cf Ex 6:3). Abraham, therefore, is part of that scattered world. We may say that he represents the point at which that world begins to respond in faith. We may perhaps detect an insight here that Israel (the church?) is nothing else than the point within the world where the call is heard and the challenge to go forward taken up.

It is hardly profitable to ask whether God actually spoke to Abraham, or whether he had what is sometimes called a spiritual experience or just a sudden brainwave.

To speak of God calling Abraham was, for the writer, an attempt to account for the conviction of divine election which had existed in Israel since the beginning. To speak of Abraham's response ('he went as the Lord had told him') was to describe what Israel's response to the new initiative must be. We should note the reticence of both Abraham and the writer. Abraham does not say anything; he just sets out into an unknown future, 'not knowing where he was to go' (Heb 11 : 8). In the same way he will set out towards the mountain to sacrifice his son, thus surrendering the only hope he could see for the future.

The promise which accompanied the call is threefold: land, posterity (nationhood) and a great name. The first is the most easily intelligible and no doubt the most original since land is what semi-nomads like Abraham need most of all. Historically this part of the promise would have been fulfilled as soon as these tribesmen had arrived in the more sparsely populated parts of the fertile land of Canaan. But the Yahwist, from whom the basic form of the narrative comes, introduces an element of tension. No sooner does Abraham come into the land than he has to leave it for Egypt, and by the end of his life all that he has secured of it is the corner of a field for a burial place. Henceforth one of the principal themes is that of *the promise deferred*.

The same is true of posterity, only here the tension becomes practically unbearable. We have already been informed that Sarai, later Sarah, is barren (11 : 30)—it is rather strange that all the ancestral mothers were barren at first—and Abraham himself is beyond the age for begetting children. When, against all the odds, a child is born, the father is at once commanded to give him up. The problems here and elsewhere for the Yahwist is one which is still very much with us: how does the man of faith think and act when God seems to be either absent or the enemy?

The Yahwist has organised all of the stories about Abraham known to him around the theme of the promise (see 12:14–16; 15:5; 17:4–5; 18:18; 22:17–18; 26:4; 28:14; 32:12; 35:11; 48:3). For him, writing during or shortly after the reign of Solomon, the promise must have seemed to have been fulfilled. With David's victories over the Philistines the conquest had at last been completed, Israel had become a great nation and her blessing radiated over the nations—Edom, Moab, Ammon, Syria—incorporated into the Davidic-Solomonic empire. But this writer is also conscious of the seeds of evil which find good soil in political institutions like monarchy, in national pride and imperialistic designs (see Gen 1–11). Later generations would have to reformulate the promise when monarchy, empire and even national identity had been swept away. But even at this earliest stage there is the belief that the promise creates history, that history is what happens between promise and fulfilment.

The wanderings of Abraham through the central hill country of Palestine seem at first sight to be rather haphazard. He arrives at Shechem, goes on to Bethel, makes his way south to the Negeb, after leaving Egypt returns to Bethel, and finally settles at Hebron. An important clue is given a little later on when Abraham is commanded to 'walk through the length and breadth of the land' (13:17). This suggests that his perambulations had a symbolic meaning—something like beating the bounds, perhaps. They indicated that the land was now his by right. We should note further that his movements pivot on three important Canaanite religious centres later frequented by the Israelites. That the forefather worshipped in these places and encountered Yahweh there would

certainly suffice to justify their further use by his descendants despite the ambiguities involved. Of the three,
Mamre-Hebron is clearly the most important for Abraham. It was here that he was buried and that his memory
was principally cherished. It was here too that David was
crowned, and we have seen that Abraham was linked
most closely with the fortunes of Judah and the Judahite
dynastic tradition.

2. Gen 12:10–13:1; 20:1–18; 26:6–11. The endangering of the ancestress

It will be sufficient to read these three passages consecutively to see that, despite differences in locale, personal
names and theological emphasis, they are parallel forms
of the same incident. Behind all three there lies an old
story told in praise of the beauty of an ancestress and the
astuteness of an ancestor. Comparison between the first
and the second shows the latter to be more theological,
explicitly at least, and ethically more sophisticated. It
also betrays some influence of prophetic thinking such as
the representation of Abraham as prophet and interces-
sor; hence the critics generally ascribe it to the Elohist
and the first to the Yahwist. But since it is more probable
that a story of this kind would be transferred from a lesser
to a greater figure than the reverse, it may well be that
the version which features Isaac and Rebekah represents
the original form. This would be confirmed by the obser-
vation that the first Abraham version seems to have been
edited into the saga-cycle (read 13:1 after 12:9).

These form-critical deductions, however, are only significant if they help us to understand why this incident
appears at this early point of the narrative. Sarai was a
beautiful woman (forget for the moment the age of sixty

five years ascribed to her by the priestly editors)—so
beautiful that there was imminent danger of her being
conscripted into the Pharaoh's harem and of her husband
being liquidated. Yet it was only through her that the
promise of posterity and nationhood could be fulfilled.
Since the retreat into Egypt had already rendered the
promise of land problematic the situation was beginning
to look desperate.

We should note that it is precisely Abraham, the bearer
of the promise, who puts its continuance in danger. The
writer probably did not share the scandal of some of the
church fathers that Abraham told a lie (though the Elohist seems worried about this too, see 20:12). He did
what most people do in a crisis—panicked and looked for
the easiest way out. Excusable as this may seem, the writer
keeps on insisting that the faith called for is of the most
demanding kind. He would have agreed with Kierkegaard that you only really believe when you are willing
to stake your life on what you believe. Abraham did not
learn all at once what he had let himself in for when he
left the security of his former life in Mesopotamia.

The denouement provides a good example of the kind
of causal thinking common in antiquity and Semitic antiquity in particular. Egypt is afflicted with plagues (this is
probably influenced by the pre-exodus plagues) and the
cause is sought for in a moral lapse since no distinction
was made between physical and moral evil. And so Abraham is able to return to Canaan and await the next turn
of events.

3. Gen 13:2–18. Separation of Lot and Abraham

Lot has already been introduced as son of the dead Haran,
nephew of Abraham and a member of the Terahite group

which migrated from Haran in Upper Mesopotamia
(11: 27–31). We realize, of course, that these kinship
bonds represent ethnic relationships in the broad sense.
As we shall see later, Lot is the ancestral 'hero' of the
Moabites and Ammonites. Despite this, however, the tradition succeeds in conveying a psychologically realistic
portrait, a genuine character study, of this individual (see
7 below).

The return to Bethel from the desert southland was,
we might say, a dramatic necessity in view of the command addressed to Abraham to look north, south, east
and west over the land promised to him (13:14). With
the increasing tension between the two groups a further
threat to the promise was developing, a return to the
disintegration of social relationships which had marked
the period under the curse illustrated in Gen 1-11. This
time Abraham's response is positive to the highest degree. He takes the initiative himself in breaking the deadlock and generously offers the younger man first choice
of pasture land. Lot gives the first of several indications
of the kind of man he is by making the easiest, the most
accommodating choice. He takes the rich land of the Jordan valley down to the Dead Sea and the Cities of the
Plain. We need not make it look worse for him by supposing that he knew the population in this latter area to
be corrupt and licentious since the writer is here preparing us for what is to follow. But in making this kind of
choice he put himself outside the community of the
promise. We shall come across many incidents of this
kind illustrating the conviction that the way of fulfilment
is not always, and perhaps not generally, the natural way.

The departure of Lot from Abraham represents a definite phase in the history of Israel's election. At the beginning the Kenites (descendants of Cain) are left aside and

the line continues through Seth (4:25). Then the generation of the flood is washed away and the line continues
through Noah. Of the sons of Noah Ham (Canaan) is
condemned and Shem is left. Abraham will have a son
by Hagar whose name is Ishmael, ancestor of Arab tribes,
but the future does not lie with them either. As the later
history of Israel will show, this conviction of election is
a terribly ambiguous, terribly dangerous idea. The prophets will purify it further by speaking of the 'remnant'
of Israel, but the tension between election and universal
mission will remain in Israel and, under changed circumstances, in the history of the christian church.

Only after Lot has departed is the promise of land and
posterity renewed and strengthend.

4. Gen 14. The battle of the nine kings. Melchize-dek and Abraham

This chapter consists of a warlike episode into which the
account of Abraham's meeting with Melchizedek of
Salem has been edited. The battle of the nine kings need
not detain us long. It is clearly quite different from the
rest of the tradition about Abraham preserved in Genesis
and has had scholars guessing for centuries. Opinions as
to its historical value vary greatly. To some it seems in-
credible that Abraham, elsewhere represented as a peaceful semi-nomad, should have routed the coalition of four
powerful kings with a band of three hundred and
eighteen followers. Others again are impressed by the
genuine-sounding names of the kings, especially that of
the Elamite king, even when they do not accept the now
obsolete identification of Amraphel with Hammurapi
king of Babylon. It has also been pointed out that this
may be a non-Israelite source since Abraham is described

as a Hebrew. Israelites never speak of themselves as Hebrews.

It is ironical, and probably appeared so to the Yahwist, that Lot had no sooner made his selfish choice than he had to be rescued by his uncle. The action takes place at the southern end of the Dead Sea where the Cities of the Plain were once located. The defeat of the local forces is due, partially at least, to the bitumen pits into which some of them fell. Again a touch of dry sarcasm. The early traditions of Israel are full of these small stories either written to explain, sometimes in a highly fanciful way, points of local interest (eg Lot's wife turned into a pillar of salt) or preserved because containing such features (as here).

Melchizedek priest-king of Salem is an unexpected intruder into this narrative. The suddenness of his appearance is to some extent responsible for his exalted place in christian tradition as precursor of Christ, without father or mother and having neither beginning of days nor end of life (Heb 7:3). Without for a moment doubting the appropriateness of later reflection on Melchizedek, we have to ask why this strange incident was put here in the first place. Melchizedek contains the same element (the name of a deity) as Adonizedek and Zadok, the former a king, the latter a priest in Jerusalem; and Salem is clearly another form of the name Jerusalem. Until its capture by David Jerusalem was a Canaanite city-state, and we know from Canaanite texts that kings also officiated as sacrificers. Ps 110, a key text for early christians in their reflection on the nature and mission of Jesus, speaks of David as 'priest for ever after the order of Melchizedek'. In view of all this, and of the nature of the Yahwist's work as a whole, we may detect David himself behind the figure of Abraham and his priest Zadok behind that of

Melchizedek. The purpose would therefore be theological but also political: to justify David's appropriation of
religious functions and, at the same time, the ascendancy
of the Zadokite priesthood which, in all probability, was
in line of descent from that of pre-Israelite Jerusalem.

We may also note that the blessing is given in the name
not of Yahweh but of 'God Most High'. This is an English
translation of El Elyon, one of the forms under which the
high god of the Canaanite pantheon is known to us from
extra-biblical texts. For anyone familiar with these texts
it is no surprise to hear him described as a creator god.
In speaking to the king of Sodom Abraham identifies
Yahweh with this deity, providing an illustration of the
many ways in which Israelite religion was enriched by
contact with other cultures.

Let us by all means reflect on this text as the starting
point for significant developments in christology and
eucharistic theology. But for the moment our purpose is
to understand the saga-cycle as a whole and how each individual passage fits into it.

5. Gen 15 and 17. Covenant with Abraham

Both the early traditions and the post-exilic theologians of
Israel backdate the covenant to Abraham. A comparison
between the two versions should be instructive.

In chapter 15 the promise of posterity and land is confirmed in the strongest terms we have found so far. Before
going on to see what this implies we should, however,
note that this chapter is not a simple, straightforward
composition from one hand. The first paragraph has to
do exclusively with the promise of posterity, whereas the
'covenant of the pieces', as it is often called, is concerned
with possession of the land. In the first paragraph it is

night, whereas a little later the sun has not yet set (15:12). A careful reading will bring to light other signs of editorial activity.

Commentators are generally agreed in finding the first traces of the Northern or Elohist source in this chapter. There is no need to discuss this in detail, but we may suggest that the assurance of eventual possession of the land by Israel after four hundred years in Egypt (15:12–16) is the Elohist parallel to the call of Abraham in 12:1–3 and that therefore the numinous experience was first thought of as taking place before Abraham set out from Mesopotamia.

In the opening verses Yahweh rejects the expedient, socially and legally acceptable at that time, according to which childless parents appointed as their heir either an adopted son or the child of a concubine. Both possibilities are set aside; the former with regard to Eliezer, the latter to Ishmael. To take a roughly parallel case, recall how often the firstborn son, the natural heir, is set aside in favour of the younger (Seth, Jacob, Saul, David, etc). It seems that in these things the unexpected always overtakes the reasonable and conventional.

The rather grisly form which the covenant-making takes is of a kind known to us from early Mesopotamian sources (the Mari tablets from the eighteenth century BC). Generally an ass was slaughtered, hacked in two, and the contracting parties passed between the severed parts of the animal. The grim symbolism was clearly understood—may the same fate befall him who reneges on his sworn oath to his partner! In the light of this the meaning of the ceremony performed here comes through with startling clarity. Yahweh alone passes between the dismembered animals and in so doing commits himself *unconditionally* to fulfilling his promises. The passing of the light between the carcasses represents for Yahweh a kind of symbolic dying. He puts his own life in the hands of Abraham and Israel whom he represents.

The covenant described in chapter 17 is, on the contrary, clearly and explicitly bilateral. It comes from the priest-theologians of a much later age and is therefore articulated much more precisely and even legalistically. For these theologians the entire history of Israel is punctuated by such covenants, beginning with Noah (9:8–17). If we first read the account of the Noahic covenant, much in the present passage will stand out more clearly. We will note, for example, that the obligations imposed concern matters to which these priestly classes ascribed great importance: in the earlier covenant food laws, in the later circumcision. Circumcision is also the identifying sign of the Abraham covenant as the rainbow is of that made with Noah. Obviously this is part of a theological scheme not too much concerned with actual historical reality. Its importance for us is the way it articulates a different understanding of how God relates to the community. This is the point to which we need to give most attention.

The idea of Yahweh committing himself to death may seem blatantly untheological, mythical or even fanciful. We might also wonder what kind of a relationship can be set up on the basis of a unilateral and unconditional commitment. Here more than elsewhere we have to remind ourselves that we are reading not a theological treatise but a unique kind of reflection on a life-history, an ongoing experience. Later on Israel will also be called upon to undergo a symbolic dying in the person of Isaac as he is led up the mountain and, indeed, in that of his father as he surrenders his last hope. Once again, it is the total experience which we are called upon to grasp.

A final note in a minor key. In 17:17 we are told that
Abraham laughed when he heard that Sarai, now Sarah,
was to have a child; as well he might since she was ninety
years old. In 18:12 Sarah herself laughed when the
mysterious visitor made the same announcement. In 21:
9–10 Ishmael is banished after Sarah sees him 'playing'
(the word has a sexual connotation) with young Isaac. In
a later episode the Philistine king sees Isaac 'playing'
with Rebekah his wife and so discovers his deception
(26:8). In all of these cases the Hebrew verb *sahaq* is
used, which is close enough to *yishaq* (Isaac) to make the
audience take the point. For what it is worth, this may
give us some idea of the art of story-telling in Israel and
temper our hunger for historical facts.

6. Gen 16. Sarah and Hagar

It seems clear from the beginning of the previous chapter
and what we read here that both Abraham and Sarah,
having come to the conclusion that the impossible does
not happen, had begun to look into alternatives. The
present chapter brings us a step closer to the point where
the tension is broken, for the time being, with the birth
of Isaac. Following a custom which seems to have been
in vogue especially among the Hurrians of Upper Mesopotamia, the couple decide to transfer rights of succession
to a son born of a slave woman. Hagar conceived but
made the mistake of pushing her luck too far. She treated
Sarah with contempt, no doubt finding a pretext in the
common assumption that barrenness, like other misfor-
tunes, was a punishment for some moral relapse. Sarah's
reaction to this was natural, predictable and entirely
within the bounds of law. Hagar had to get out.

The meeting with a heavenly visitant by a well in the

desert is of a kind found everywhere in ancient literature. He gives Hagar a threefold message: that she must return to her mistress, that from her will come a great multitude, that she will give birth to a wild and uncontrollable son. The last two refer to Ishmael as the ancestral 'hero' of Arab tribes well known to many of the tribes which later formed Israel. The first is meant to prepare us for the further expulsion described in 21:8–21. Over and above this the incident contains a place-aetiology of the kind so frequent in the old testament. It provides a popular explanation of how the well in the Sinai peninsula called 'the well of the one who lives and sees' got its name. We shall learn later that there was a sanctuary here to which the local inhabitants later attached the memory of the patriarch Isaac.

It might not be out of place to add a brief remark at this point on the role of women in these ancient traditions and in the Yahwist work in particular. The modern reader may well be disturbed at the frequency with which woman is represented as temptress, leading man to ruinous courses. For the Yahwist it seems that evil establishes its first beachhead through women—the first woman in Gen 3 and the 'daughters of men' in the mythical fragment in Gen 6:1–4. The evils that beset Jacob are ascribed to the foreign wives of Esau (26:34–35; 27:46) and the ancestral mothers themselves are often described as unscrupulous or lacking in deep faith as they doggedly pursue their own ends. It is not too difficult to put forward explanations of this attitude, especially in the Yahwist work. There was the experience of the early monarchy—David's adultery with Bathsheba, whom we can hardly consider as innocent and forced to comply against her will, and the foreign women of Solomon. There was the influence of the wisdom-teachers in whom this theme runs strongly (suffice it to read Prov 1–9) and, above all, the role of women in Canaanite rituals with which all were familiar. To explain is not, however, to justify, much less to identify with; but may we not pluck up enough courage to ask whether the Yahwist does not provide a corrective against the depreciation of sexual differentiation in our culture whether at the popular level or in the work of, say, Simone de Beauvoir? Whatever the answer, some ambiguities may well be clarified if we think it worth while to take up the challenge.

7. Gen 18–19. Theophany at Mamre. The fate of Sodom and Gomorrah

Behind the first narrative which takes place at Mamre there lies a theologically unsophisticated story, similar to many told in antiquity of a god appearing incognito or otherwise to a pious devotee. In a way typical of the Yahwist it has become the framework for a further renewal of the promise while retaining much local colour, interesting detail and movement. There seems to be, in addition, the intention of emphasizing the lavish hospitality of Abraham in contrast to the behaviour of the depraved inhabitants of Sodom and Gomorrah.

The confusion between the three and the one, which led several church fathers to read into it a prefiguration of the Trinity, may be due to the conflation of this theophany story with the account of the destruction of the two cities by two angels. The problem is neatly solved by leaving Yahweh behind with Abraham (since it was unthinkable that he could be the object of homosexual aggression) while the two angels in human form go on to the Cities of the Plain as agents of divine judgment.

Though it would be wrong to overemphasise it, we

may find in Sarah's disbelief of the word of Yahweh and subsequent lie an illustration of what was said in the previous section on the role of the woman. For the Yahwist, the fundamental human attitude is a trusting so strong and deep that it can lead to a total life-investment. Abraham is for him the embodiment of this attitude: he believed Yahweh, and it was reckoned to him as righteousness (15:6). To Sarah's incredulous laugh the only answer is: 'Is anything too hard for Yahweh?' (18:14).

The narrative about Sodom and Gomorrah provides a particularly tragic example of what faulty exegesis and unsound hermeneutics can lead to—in this case it is no exaggeration to say that it has contributed substantially to the savage treatment of the homosexual and the imposition of the death penalty for homosexual practice in so-called christian countries. Let us leave aside for the moment 'what actually happened' and try to get some perspective on how the story is told. For one thing, there is an air of unreality about it. All the people of the city, young and old, *to the last man*, take part in this attempted gang-rape (19:4). This leaves Peyton Place well in the shade. We might compare the account of Ham's immodesty (or worse) with respect to his incapacitated father in 9:20–24 where the precautions taken by the other brothers are ludicrously exaggerated. The same kind of exaggeration, a perfectly valid technique of the storyteller, appears in the story of the crime of the people of Gibeah, Saul's city (Jgs 19) which is practically a double of the Sodom and Gomorrah story. Here, among other things, the levite cuts his violated concubine into twelve parts and sends them round the twelve tribes. Some scholars think this may be an unfriendly skit on Saul, and we would have equal right to suggest that the present chapter is a skit on the (for the Israelite) disgusting Canaanite practice of male cultic prostitution. The Canaanites called these cultic persons 'holy ones' but the Israelites called them 'dogs'.

If this seems far-fetched read on to the last paragraph of the chapter where the story of Lot's drunkenness and the incest of his daughters is told. As is clear from the conclusion, this is a satire directed against Moab and Ammon, two old enemies of the Israelites. We are not suggesting that the writer thought there was anything very funny about drunkenness, homosexual outrage or incest. But his purpose was other than that of moralist or fire-and-brimstone preacher.

There is no reason to doubt that some settlements lying in what is now the southern arm of the Dead Sea were destroyed by earthquake. This region lies on a fault which goes down to the Red Sea and penetrates deeply into East Africa. Many stories of a popular nature must have grown up around the destruction of these cities. Lot's wife and the pillar of salt would be one of these. Even before the time of the great prophets it had become a paradigm, almost *the* paradigm, of divine judgement.

It would certainly be of interest, finally, to reflect on the figure of Lot as he is presented to us in the tradition. He belongs to the community of blessing but almost in spite of himself. He is the kind of person whose goodness is negative and uncreative, from whom one cannot expect anything very much. When we first meet him he is at loggerheads with Abraham, does nothing to break the deadlock, and makes a selfish choice of the best land. Almost at once he has to be rescued by Abraham, and it is the power of Abraham's intercession which saves him from going down with the doomed cities (19:29). He has to be almost forcibly removed from the city by the two divine emissaries, both he and his wife linger as they leave, he is still bargaining for a good deal for himself almost as the hot ash is beginning to fall and does not, after all this, accept the option offered him of living in Zoar. He does not wait very long before throwing his two daughters, already engaged to marry, to the sex-crazed mob, an action which is repaid him with vengeance in the double incest which follows. He is not wicked, but what goodness he has is brittle and superficial. He is a man on whom no one can rely.

8. Gen 21. The birth of Isaac and the saving of Ishmael

The tension throughout most of the Abraham cycle arises out of the question whether Sarah, against every natural calculation, will have a child. We are reminded continually that she is barren and in any case too old to have children. She has been in danger of disappearing from the scene on more than one occasion and different expedients have been tried to keep the promise of posterity alive by legal fictions in use at that time. At Mamre she was told she would conceive but did not believe it. Now the impossible happens and the child is born.

The name Isaac is again explained with reference to laughing but in a way different from the other aetiologies we have seen (5 above). Here it is a good omen, as indeed it has to be.

The ejection of Hagar and Ishmael looks like a parallel to the incident in chapter 16 (6 above). It contains one memorable and touching scene as the slave woman prepares to die having first put her little son out of sight under a bush. Ishmael is to share in the blessing of Abraham but the promise is not to continue through him.

The last section of this chapter is a kind of postscript

to the incident described in the previous chapter involving a Philistine king named Abimelech. It seems to have grown out of an attempt to explain the name and origin of Beersheba, an important religious centre in the south of Judah to which later generations attached the memory of Isaac. In Hebrew *Beersheba* could mean either 'the well of the seven' or 'the well of swearing' (an oath, understood). It could also mean neither of these, but this was of no great concern to the writer. At this sanctuary the high god El was worshipped under yet another designation which in the course of time passed over to Yahweh. We have to remind ourselves that the patriarchs did not worship Yahweh, the god of the federation. They worshipped different deities who only in the course of time came to be identified with Yahweh 'the god of Abraham, Isaac and Jacob'.

Since the Philistines only arrived in the land to which they gave their name at the beginning of the twelfth century, it is difficult to know what a Philistine king is doing there several centuries earlier. The anachronism may be explained by reference to David's relations with the Philistines during the reign of Saul since he too entered into league with them. This would be one more example of the close ties between the presentation of Abraham in the tradition and the emergent Davidic monarchy.

9. Gen 22:1–19. The binding of Isaac

If we dig down beneath the surface of this story we shall find several superimposed layers of meaning. It may well have been intended indirectly as a reprobation of the practice of human sacrifice, especially infant sacrifice, examples of which are known from the old testament. It

could at the same time have served as an explanation of
the custom of 'redeeming' the firstborn by means of an
animal sacrifice. The original ending of the story (22 : 14)
also shows that it was intended to explain the name of a
particularly numinous mountain shrine, though the
location is no longer easy to reconstruct. At the time of
the Chronicler (the post-exilic period) Moriah was understood to be Jerusalem; hence the tradition that the near-
sacrifice took place on the temple area. But these traditions easily migrate from one place to another, and earlier
religious centres were deliberately downgraded once
Jerusalem became the state sanctuary.

None of this, however, is of primary importance for the
interpretation of the story as it now stands in the context
in which it has been placed. We have seen that the tension building up from the beginning was at last broken
with the birth of the promised son. Now, just a few years
later, Abraham is asked to give him up. Yahweh tests
Abraham only after he has committed himself to death
by passing between the dismembered animals. Now
Abraham is tested to the point of death: the death of his
son and the death of his own hopes. Kierkegaard said that
when God calls a man he calls him to die. This is the
symbolic dying that Abraham faced as he climbed the
mountain.

The story is told in a way worthy of this crucial
moment in the unfolding drama. Whether or not we
must attribute it to the Elohist (this has been until recently the generally accepted view), it is by common con-
sent one of the masterpieces of Hebrew prose. In the
first chapter of his *Mimesis*, Erich Auerbach brings out
some of the inner dynamism of the narrative by con-
trasting it with Homer's account of the homecoming of
Odysseus: the almost unbearable silence of Abraham,

the expressive use of detail, the emphasis on time rather than space, the tension and pathos (the reader knows the outcome but the actors do not). It is not until the last moment, when the knife is raised in the air, that the tension is broken. As John Osborne's Luther says, if God had blinked Isaac would have been dead.

Though the story obviously centres on Abraham, later Jewish tradition has shifted the theological emphasis on to the figure of Isaac. Isaac knows what is at stake, he accepts his death freely and allows himself to be bound on the altar of sacrifice; which explains why the incident is generally referred to in Jewish sources as the *akedah* or binding of Isaac. In thus freely submitting to death and receiving his life back from the hands of God, Isaac is the figure of Israel in its life of faith. In the same role he is the pattern of existential meaning behind the theology of sacrifice in judaism and has clearly, if indirectly, influenced christian thinking about the eucharist.

These insights which we take from judaism are invaluable and ought to be taken up and discussed. But we must re-affirm at this point that, in the present context, this is a story about Abraham and must be understood as such. It is, in fact, the climax of the Abraham cycle. After this point his mission is fulfilled and there is nothing more for him to do but prepare for his death.

10. Gen 22:20–25:11. Epilogue. Last dispositions of Abraham. His death

The only important things which remain to be said about Abraham are his dispositions to procure a burial place and to find a suitable wife for his heir. We shall consider the former here (chapter 23) but the latter (chapter 24) really belongs to the history of Isaac and will be discussed later. We may take it that Abraham died before the return of the servant with Rebekah since Isaac is now by himself (24:62–67).

Sarah died at a ripe old age at Hebron and Abraham set about bargaining with the Hittites, 'the people of the land', with a view to purchasing a burial place for her, himself and his heirs. To understand what follows it is essential to remember that though Abraham lives in or near Hebron he is an alien. An alien could not be a property owner and was, in general, politically disadvantaged.

The negotiations are given in detail and provide an interesting and even amusing example of how orientals bargain to this day. Abraham wants to invest in real estate but this is just what the Hittites do not want since it would give him equal political standing and might prove to be the thin end of the wedge. So they answer politely, addressing him as a 'mighty prince', and assure him free access to their own burial places. After suitable preparation, however, Abraham makes his concrete proposal, well thought out in advance, and insists politely on an outright purchase. What happens at this stage, when Ephron offers the field and cave for free, is not altogether clear. Some think he was offering them as a feudal holding since something akin to feudalism was known to the Hittites and Hurrians (the 'Hittites' here were probably Hurrians). But it seems more likely that this was just the customary style of polite bargaining which no one was expected to take seriously. In any case, he at once throws off the trifling figure of four hundred shekels (several thousands of pounds)—people like you and me don't need to haggle over such details. This figure Abraham at once accepts, probably to Ephron's great astonishment, and the deal is closed.

In this way Abraham obtained his only stake in the
land of promise—a burial place, nothing more. Here
he buried his wife, here he himself was buried (25:9–
10) together with most of the other ancestors and their
wives (49:29–32). The alleged site is now inside the
mosque of Abraham Friend of God at Hebron. The
tombs are covered in rich drapes: red for the men, blue
for the women.

The later Priestly source gives us official notice of
Abraham's death (25:7–11) together with other diverse
bits of genealogical information: the family of Nahor,
Abraham's brother (22:20–24), Abraham's descendants
by Keturah (25:1–6), other Arab tribes descended from
Ishmael (25:12–18). These are the product of an over-
tidy mentality and need hardly detain us. Everything
of importance has already been said.

Questions for discussion

*(Though discussion will no doubt go on throughout, it
seems best to put these suggested questions at the end
of each cycle to avoid breaking up the flow of the
narrative)*

*1. What light does the Abraham cycle throw on the
meaning of faith and election (calling)? Is there anything important here which we have lost sight of? Read
the new testament references to Abraham, especially
Rom 4 and Heb 11:8–22, and comment on them.*

*2. Much is being written these days about the mean-
ing of hope for the christian, especially with reference
to possible dialogue with marxists. What insights does
the Abraham cycle provide for this question? How do
the biblical writers solve the problem of the promise
deferred?*

3. Do these stories imply that the man of faith is committed to live in insecurity?

4. Attempt a character-study of Lot and try to answer the question: is this a universal type?

5. How can we speak meaningfully today of providence, the hidden activity of God within history?

6. What does the almost perverse rejection of socially acceptable expedients tell us about the manner of God's acting in history? (see especially sections 5, 6 and 8).

7. Comment on the role of women in these narratives and assess the extent to which they have influenced present-day attitudes, especially those of churchmen.

8. What contribution does Gen 22 (section 9) make towards an understanding of sacrifice? May we still speak of the eucharist as sacrificial in the light of this understanding?

2
The Isaac cycle
Gen 21:1–35:29

3. Gen 21:1–35:29. Finding a bride for Isaac

Isaac is born amid a cloud of punning references to his name (21:1–7 and 5 above) and his death is recorded rather laconically towards the end of a long sequence of narratives about his heir (35:29). Between these points, however, there are very few incidents which centre directly on him. The *akedah* or binding of Isaac is, as we have seen, definitely an Abraham story despite the change of emphasis in Jewish tradition. Apart from this, he never really comes alive off the pages.

Towards the end of his life Abraham sends his most trusted servant back to the homeland of the ancestors to find a bride for Isaac. The emphasis both here and in the somewhat similar story about Jacob's search for a bride (3 below) is on the danger of 'mixed marriages'. This theme is strongly stressed by many of the theologians of Israel and especially by the Yahwist. We come across it not only here but also in the references to the foreign wives of Esau (26:34–35; 27:46) and the baneful effects of Judah's marriage to a Canaanite girl (38:2–11). We recall that David's troubles began with Bathsheba, married to a Hittite, and Solomon's with the introduction of foreign women into his harem. Much later Ezekiel will, by implication, ascribe the apostasy of Jerusalem to racial intermarriage (Ezek 16:3).

It is hardly necessary to say that the dangers of this emphasis will be more apparent to us than its advantages or necessity. We cannot go into this in detail, but two remarks ought to be made by way of clarifying the issue. The first is that the idea of a Hebrew race ethnically 'pure' from its origins is a myth. Though predominantly of one strain, the early Hebrews included different elements and were not even exclusively semitic. The emphasis here is not really racial at all but cultural. The danger to be avoided was cultural (and therefore religious) assimilation with the more sophisticated Canaanites, leading inevitably to the submergence of a sense of unique destiny. The second is that Israel still had to learn through her own experience, interpreted by her prophets and wise men, that her destiny and mission were in view of a community transcending racial and political barriers. Something of this is present in the Yahwist's work but it took the experience of centuries to bring it to full consciousness.

The story of the servant's journey and the idyllic scene by the well are excellently narrated in the slow-paced way characteristic of the best of early Hebrew prose. The Yahwist seems fond of chance encounters: the servant with Rebekah at the well, Rebekah with Isaac in the Negeb. Only, if one has but eyes to see with, nothing happens by chance. It may be difficult for us today to speak with conviction of abandonment to providence. The term too easily connotes an abdication of personal responsibility and a lazy compliance with received religious ideas. The servant's prayer before seeing Rebekah and his thanksgiving afterwards imply something very different from this: a conviction that a meaning exists and a strong determination to discover it. As always up till now, the promise takes on reality only when it finds men strong enough to assume responsibility for its fulfilment.

The first girl who turns up at the well turns out to be the grand-daughter of Nahor brother of Abraham. She is unmarried but gives evidence of excellent qualities as a prospective wife: willingness to help, spontaneous generosity and hospitality. Laban her brother, who seems to be in charge of the household, is from a different mould. He is quick to notice that his visitor is both wealthy and generous. Subsequently he will exploit Jacob to the limit, only to be finally outwitted by him. There may, perhaps, be some instruction for us in observing characters like Laban and Lot who are not evil but whose lives are ruined by self-interest.

6. Gen 26:12–33. Isaac's dealings with the Philistines

The story of the birth of Esau and Jacob and the handing over of the birthright belong to the long series of narratives about the two sons and can therefore be passed over for the moment.

Nobody really knows what to make of Abimelech king of the Philistines with whom both Abraham and Isaac have to live in a state of uneasy co-existence. Unless the historians are in for a big surprise as a result of future discoveries, it seems out of the question that Philistines could have settled in any part of Palestine much before the Israelites, who began to take over in the thirteenth century. It is also unlikely, as we saw earlier, that Abimelech would have made the same mistake with Rebekah as he had with Sarah; hence the two

narratives (20 : 1–18 and 26 : 1–11) must be variants of
the same incident. It would be a veiled warning against
intermarriage or any other form of accommodation with
the Philistines who were, for the Israelites, just as im-
moral and sexually promiscuous as the Canaanites. It
may be recalled that one of the causes of Samson's down-
fall was marriage to a Philistine girl.

The same may well be true of the covenant or treaty
which both Abraham and Isaac made with Abimelech
(21 : 22–34 and 26 : 26–33). In both cases the cause of
contention which led to the treaty was the vital question
of the ownership of wells in the Negeb or southland.
This has drawn to itself all sorts of small-scale local traditions concerning the names of particular wells (26 :
17–22) including a rash of etymologies purporting to
explain the name Beersheba (21 : 25–31 and 26 : 32–33).
As suggested earlier, much of this may reflect David's
dealings with the Philistines. These too implied a treaty
and had as their scenario the steppeland of the south
below Jerusalem.

What for our immediate purpose is important here is
the solemn renewal of the promise to Isaac (26 : 1–11)
and the ongoing effects of the *beraka* (blessing) of Abraham (26 : 12–14). That this blessing has to do exclusively
with 'material things'—land, crops, cattle, all that meant
wealth for the people of that time—might seem to put
the whole enterprise on a rather low level for us who
are accustomed to think in terms of spiritual goals. Similarly, the emphasis on political success—in this case with
respect to the Philistines—might seem to indicate a
phase of religious awareness now superseded. If this is
our attitude we may be in danger of missing the point.
Throughout the patriarchal narratives, and in fact
throughout the old testament as a whole, especially the

prophetic writings, there is a stubborn refusal to extrapolate into a timeless world where everything will be different from the present. Throughout the long history of its interpretation and re-interpretation the promise is never detached from concrete, historical realities. It never becomes 'spiritual' as opposed to political, economic, sociological etc. It is always concerned essentially and exclusively with the future of the earth and the creation of a genuine human community. This is an important truth which we have been in danger of losing and which these stories, when correctly interpreted, can recall.

The death of Isaac occurs only after Jacob's return from a long absence in Mesopotamia (35:29) despite the fact that his deathbed blessings are given more than twenty years previously. But at this point he falls out of the story and from now on Jacob alone is the centre of interest.

1. What do we mean by providence? In what way, if at all, can we speak today of God acting in history, in human affairs?

2. Is the concrete, this-worldly nature of the promise cancelled out by the christian fulfilment? In other words, is there here a direct line of continuity between old and new testament or must the promise to the patriarchs be interpreted typologically?

3

The Jacob cycle
Gen 25:19–50:14

1. Gen 25:19–34. The birth of Esau and Jacob. The sale of the birthright

It is, of course, impossible to read this as in any sense of the term an historical record. Everything about the origins of the great ancestor must be out of the ordinary. He is, in a way, conceived miraculously. Rebekah, like all the ancestral mothers, was barren and could only conceive by the power of God after Isaac had interceded for her. Here, as in the story of the virgin birth, the key issue is that the community represented respectively by Jacob (Israel) and the Christ lives solely by the power and the grace of God. The destiny of Israel is also prefigured by the struggle in the womb. This warns us right from the start that the life of Jacob prefigures or, better, recapitulates the historical existence and destiny of the community which bears his name.

The oracular saying in 25:23 draws our attention to the immediate significance of this incident and the one which follows. Right into the post-exilic period Edom remained the arch-enemy of Israel. Though it reached nationhood earlier than its neighbour (see Gen 36:31) it was conquered by Israel and incorporated into the Davidic empire, though later it regained independence. To get some idea of Israelite hatred of Edom as late as the exile all one has to do is read the final verses of Ps 137 ('by the waters of Babylon').

The birth story is built on a collection of popular etymologies of the synonyms Edom and Seir. In Hebrew the former can mean 'red' and the latter 'hairy'. The Edom-red motif also dominates the story about the lost birthright, a story which is so familiar that we may not notice how ridiculous it is. Esau is represented as a crude, brainless type, a drooling idiot who, when overcome by hunger, surrenders his status and basic rights for a bowl of blood soup. Clearly we have here a satire or skit on Edom, one example of a *genre* at which the early Israelites seem to have been particularly adept. The characterization of Esau as hunter and Jacob as tent-dweller (therefore shepherd and goatherd) must also be explained by reference to Edom and Israel in the early period. We may compare it with the different occupations of Cain and Abel in Gen 4, especially since the former is the ancestral hero of the Kenites, a tribe which was at home in Edom.

The name Jacob, which is known to us from non-biblical sources, is also given a popular etymology. It is probably a short form of a name which means 'may God protect', but here it is given the meaning 'he who takes by the heel, he who supplants'.

2. Gen 27:1–45. Deathbed blessing on Jacob and Esau

We have already learned that Isaac favoured Esau while Jacob was his mother's boy. In the incident which now follows, Rebekah shows herself to be resourceful, even unscrupulous, in the pursuit of Jacob's interests. She plays a role similar in some respects to that of Bathsheba who worked so hard to get her son Solomon on the throne. Rebekah is the architect of the cruel deceit practised on her husband and all Jacob has to do is to fall in with her plan.

We will probably detect here the same rather ludicrous element as in the story of the red pottage or blood soup. As if anyone not in his dotage—and Isaac was not that far gone—could have mistaken goat's hair for the hands and neck of his son, no matter how hirsute he may have been! It seems that here again the joke is against Esau, the human gorilla who was all brawn and no brain. Only this time it does not quite come off. The sympathies of the perceptive reader are soon drawn to him and against the scheming mother-and-son team. To practise this kind of deceit on an old man nearly blind is not really very funny, quite apart from the great religious importance given to these last blessings of the father. When Esau, having discovered what had happened, lets out his great and bitter cry, when he lifts up his voice and weeps, comedy has already turned to pathos.

It is important to note that Jacob comes out of this very badly indeed. He has no character of his own and, apparently, little moral conviction. He is even prepared to indulge in a little blasphemy ('Yahweh your God granted me success') to help the scheme along. He seems to be completely under his mother's thumb. It is only by taking note of this that we can appreciate the meaning of the experience and suffering which is to follow. For although Rebekah unthinkingly assumes responsibility for the curse which may come of it, it is Jacob who will have to pay the price—the heavy price of twenty years' exile from home.

The political significance of the episode is brought

out quite clearly in the blessings pronounced by the father. That on Jacob (Israel) makes more explicit the promise to Abraham of fertility and nationhood and presupposes the realisation of the blessing in the Davidic empire. The oracle pronounced over Esau (Edom) is even more explicit since it presupposes the temporary subjugation of that kingdom by David and its regained independence towards the end of Solomon's reign.

We referred to these as deathbed blessings since this is what they seem to be. Yet Isaac still has at least twenty years of life in front of him since he survived to see his son Jacob return from the long exile. Either he was a tougher old man than anyone suspected or this may be just one of many inconsistencies which the editors did not bother to iron out.

3. Gen 27:46–29:14. Jacob finds Rachel

The journey of Jacob to Mesopotamia, his long stay of twenty years there and the return to Canaan form the nucleus of the Jacob cycle. The journey seems to be the archetypal biblical theme. This journey was a regression since the direction was the reverse of that of Abraham; but Jacob's re-entry into Canaan, marked by wonderful and numinous experiences as it was, signalled a new and decisive stage in the forward movement of the history.

The initiative for the journey is attributed to both Rebekah and Isaac, which may signify the editing together of two distinct sources. In both cases the reason given is the need to avoid marriage with a native woman (see 3 above). The blessing bestowed by Isaac (28:3–4) may well be a double of the deathbed blessing obtained by deceit; there is at least no reference to this latter incident here.

The outset of the journey was marked by a numinous experience at the ancient Canaanite sanctuary of Bethel. Here the deity, who revealed himself as Yahweh, God of the fathers, promised to be with Jacob and to bring him back to the land of promise. As soon as he was within reach of Canaan on his return he once again saw the angels of God (32:1), encountered Yahweh (32:22–32) and, again at Bethel, was assured of the promise and was given the name Israel (35:9–12). These numinous, sacred or cultic experiences seem to have the purpose of bringing out the inner significance of the ostensibly secular happenings in which Jacob is involved. This would suggest that 'sacred' and 'profane' are concerned with one and the same reality. At any rate, we would do well to consider how incidents like the theophany at Bethel interpenetrate the ongoing history.

Jacob's experience at Bethel may reflect the ancient and well-attested practice of sleeping in a sanctuary in order to have divine guidance or enlightenment through a dream. What he saw in his dream was not a ladder—since it would be difficult even for angels to move up and down a ladder simultaneously—but a series of steps like those on the stepped pyramids or ziggurats of Mesopotamia. That the image is that of a ziggurat or something like it is confirmed by his final exclamation: 'house of God' is a literal translation of Beth-el and 'gate of heaven' of the name 'Babylon', in or near which city the ziggurats were built.

The dedication and naming of this sanctuary obviously has something to do with the fact that Bethel became the state-sanctuary of the northern kingdom. As such it is well known to us from the history and the

prophets, especially Amos and Hosea. It was here that
the memory of Jacob was especially cherished and many
of the traditions about him formed and preserved. The
action of the great ancestor was obviously understood
to have legitimised and sanctioned the use of this ancient
religious centre by the Israelites.

The renewal of the promise came when most needed,
at the last stop in the land of Canaan. For the next
twenty years Jacob had to learn to live without visible
reassurances, resist the temptation of making a life of it
in the land of his forefathers, and hope continually for
a future which seemed to be constantly deferred. This
was to be the testing time and we shall see how he came
out of it.

Upon arrival in Haran the scene of the servant and
Rebekah at the well was repeated, this time with Jacob
and Rachel. She too turned up at the right moment. The
writer dwells on the prodigious strength of the hero
who, prompted no doubt by the near presence of Rachel,
removed single-handedly the stone from the well which
it normally took several shepherds to roll away. After
failing to get rid of the shepherds, Jacob went ahead and
kissed Rachel unashamedly, in defiance of social con-
vention—another revealing indication of character. This
kiss so worried Luther that he suggested it must be a
textual error.

4. Gen 29:15–30:24. The sons of Jacob

To the modern reader who has no dogmatic axe to
grind, this section, as others in the saga of the forefathers,
will present some rather strange and improbable features. It may seem odd, for example, that Jacob should
be prepared to wait fourteen years for his bride. Early

marriage is practically mandatory for orientals, especially for girls, and we may want to ask how such an impulsive man as Jacob could have lived in close proximity to the woman he loved for such a long time without doing something more drastic to break the moratorium imposed by his mean and calculating relative. It may seem even odder that he should have been taken in by the atrocious deceit of Laban who put Leah in Rachel's place on the wedding night. The reasons given by the commentators: that the bride was veiled (did she remain veiled all night?), that Jacob was too drunk to notice (how drunk do you have to be to marry the wrong girl?), that the two were alike (this is contradicted by 29:17)— all of these are really quite insufficient to account for it. The simplest answer seems to be the one already suggested: that this was for Jacob the testing time; that the community willed by God had to be built on a well-tried and tested rock foundation; that nothing enduring is built without great suffering.

On a less sublime level, we have here the beginning of a long battle of wits between the two men, a battle fought with no holds barred. Laban will eventually get the worst of the exchange, but in the meantime he exacted a heavy price. It is clear that the keynote of the whole Jacob cycle of stories is struggle, and this was obviously intended as the main lesson for Israel.

The rest of the narrative concerns the birth of Jacob's sons, the ancestral 'heroes' of the twelve tribes (the birth of Benjamin, the twelfth, is recorded in 35:16–18). The name of each of the sons is given a popular etymology which does not necessarily inform us on the real etymology of the name or the person who bears it or the tribe named after him. The fact that some of the tribal names are geographical rather than personal is enough to reveal the artificiality of this genealogical technique. The patriarchal narratives, we repeat, come from the twelve-tribal federation or amphictyony (a term borrowed from the Greeks). We cannot emphasise too much that their principal purpose is to articulate the consciousness of election and the spiritual destiny of this particular community. If we miss this we cannot really understand why these stories were written and what they intended to convey.

Once we accept this, the present narrative will be easier to understand. The distinction between the Leah and Rachel tribes may point to an earlier six-tribal league later augmented by the important tribes which settled in the centre of the country north of Jerusalem. Understandably, the Jacob-saga gives most importance to the sons of Rachel, namely, Joseph and Benjamin. Joseph corresponds to Ephraim and Manasseh (see chapter 48) and Benjamin, meaning 'southerner', constituted the southern province of these 'Joseph tribes'. It was among these tribes that Jacob assumed the great importance which he has in the tradition.

The little episode of the mandrakes found by Reuben is a typically colourful addition to the narrative. The use of this popular aphrodisiac served Leah's purpose well. Rachel wanted them too, and needed them more than Leah since she was barren. But this human expedient, like so many others in these narratives, was set aside, and she gave birth to Joseph only when God remembered her and gave her the gift of fruitfulness.

5. Gen 30:25–31:16. Jacob and Laban

Jacob had already served fourteen years for his two wives. During this time both he and his wives had, to all intents and purposes, become the slaves of Laban. He had no political status, no economic security, and the promise made to him at Bethel seemed more distant of fulfilment than ever. It is clear that legally he could not leave the employment of Laban and return to Canaan; and Laban had everything to gain by making him stay where he was.

We must not suppose that Laban, in asking Jacob to name his wages, was giving proof of any disinterested generosity. He was not that kind of person. It emerges clearly that, for the writer, Laban was one of those characters who are prepared to exploit the goodness of others and manipulate the law to their own advantage—in this case, even when it concerned his own daughters (31 : 15). He is a good illustration of the fact, often overlooked, that money and possessions are more dangerous than sexual pleasure, anger or the other passions, since they more easily wound the capacity to accept others. Laban stands for all those who *use* other people.

The time had come, however, for Jacob to turn the tables on Laban. He agreed to continue as his herdsman but on conditions laid down by himself, conditions which Laban accepted since they seemed to his advantage. His plan which involved pre-natal visual conditioning, was of course quite unscientific—rather like the pregnant woman who plays the piano in the hope that her offspring will be a musical genius. But, for the writer it worked, and that was all that mattered. It was even authenticated by a divinely inspired dream. By this and other means Jacob became more prosperous and Laban, and his sons began to feel threatened. It was evidently time for Jacob to leave and it was not difficult for him to persuade his wives, who were the legal property of their father, to accompany him.

The decision to return, as with all important turning points in the history, cannot be purely casual or fortuitous. The voice which had spoken to him twenty years previously in the sanctuary of Bethel came to him again and told him to return to the land of his birth. The end of the waiting period was drawing near.

6. Gen 31:17–55. Jacob's return: the first stage

It was suggested earlier that the journey is a basic biblical motif and one which is found throughout the literature of the world. It would be interesting to compare the journeys of Abraham and Jacob with other archetypal examples of the motif; for example, that of Gilgamesh (see 29 and 35 above) or of Ulysses, operative after three thousand years in the work of Joyce (*Ulysses*) and Kazantzakis (*The Odyssey : A Modern Sequel*) among others. In each case the meaning has to be found on the level of religious symbolism.

The journey on which Jacob now prepares to embark is an exodus like that of Abraham (the same starting point) and of the Israelites from Egypt. Like the latter, Jacob had to leave surreptitiously and only after careful planning. Like them he too was pursued and saved only by an extraordinary intervention of Yahweh. Most important, Jacob was also escaping from an intolerable situation which involved economic and spiritual slavery. As long as he remained with Laban he could not be his own man or exist as a free person. This escape from economic, political and spiritual slavery is *the* biblical archetype of salvation.

By careful planning he got a headstart of three days on his kinsman, crossed the Euphrates and headed for Gilead in the Transjordan area. But you don't make

spectacular progress driving cattle, sheep and goats before you, so it was no surprise when Laban overtook
him after a week of hot pursuit across the Syrian desert.
He accused Jacob not only of leaving his service without
permission but also and especially of stealing his household gods. This last was obviously a major concern and
it is only recently that we have discovered why. According to customary law operative in Upper Mesopotamia
at that time, possession of the *terafim* or household gods
(small figurines probably made of baked clay) signified
the right of succession to the family property. Jacob was
therefore being accused of usurping the position of heir
and making a bid for the wealth which Laban's family
had accumulated. We must suppose that Jacob really
did not know that his wife had stolen the *terafim*; hence
the dramatic tension for the audience when he unwit-
tingly condemned her to death. We may compare a similar dramatic moment in the story of Joseph (Gen 44:
9) and in the history of Saul (1 Sam 14:24-46).

Laban's desperate search for his household gods is
told with a sly sarcasm of a kind often illustrated in these
stories. According to an age-old taboo which has passed
into levitical law a woman was ritually unclean during
her period. The storyteller was certainly playing it for
laughs when he thought up this conclusion to the story
of the idols of such vital importance to the pagans, and
to the avaricious Laban in particular. At this point all
of Jacob's resentment came out, but the contention was
finally settled by a sworn treaty sealed by a common
meal, as was the custom. After this Jacob was at last free
to enter once again into the land which had been
promised to him.

7. Gen 32–33. Jacob's return: the second stage

The meeting with the angels of God meant that the land was now near. They were, so to speak, patrols sent out by the Lord of armies (cf the rather puzzling episode in Josh 5:13–15). Beneath the briefly narrated incident run the undertones of *struggle* which is the key-concept in the Jacob cycle. The hero's struggle, which began in the womb, had been going on for twenty years in a foreign land and was now to reach its climax and outcome. He now had to reconquer the land, a presage of the conquest carried out by the twelve tribes descended from him. At the risk of misunderstanding, we might say that this return was a 'spiritual' conquest. Jacob had first to find strength in himself to bear the weight of the promise. He returned to Canaan a different man from the one that left it, a man schooled by the experience and suffering of twenty years in exile.

The main problem was Esau, the brother dispossessed by deceit. Orientals have good memories for both favours and insults and Jacob had good reason to fear, even after such a lapse of time. Here as elsewhere, however, the narrative cannot be read on the purely personal level. Jacob's fear, his precautionary action and the eventual peaceful outcome almost certainly reflect the experience of the Israelites about to pass through Seir (Edom) on their way to Canaan (here one might look at Deut 2:4–8). The two companies must have something to do with the place-name Mahanaim (literally, 'two camps') in Transjordan, a city which was to play an important part in the history of the early monarchy. Jacob's elaborate precautionary measures were so successful that the painful subject of the birthright did not even arise.

The mysterious wrestling match which took place at the ford over the Jabbok river can be read in all kinds of different ways. We are only told that 'a man', who turns out to be more than a man, began it, that he was obviously losing, and that he only avoided defeat by a foul preternaturally executed. The original layer of the story may have concerned a night demon (like the ghost of Hamlet's father he had to leave by daybreak) who in the popular imagination haunted a particularly treacherous river crossing. There is also the usual rash of aetiologies or popular origin-stories: the Israelite taboo against eating the sciatic nerve, the name Penuel or Peniel which means 'God's face' and, most important, the name Israel interpreted to fit the story (no one knows the origin of the name but the most probable guess is 'let El (God) shine').

Some commentators seem to imagine that they have exhausted the meaning of a story like this once they have fastened on to one or other of the popular or folk elements involved. Nothing could be further from the truth. May we not find here the attempt of the community itself to come to an understanding of its own destiny—not to settle down, not to define its existence and purpose in terms of the goals pursued by 'the nations round about', not to come to easy terms with life, but to engage in a struggle 'with God and with men' (32 : 28) in which its own identity, signified by the name, is at stake? The struggle with God, the loving adversary, ends in union signified by the blessing. The struggling with men has immediate reference to the encounter with Esau which also ends in reconciliation. It is not too difficult to see how the Israel of a later day could have understood this as symbolic of its own destiny and purpose.

The final stage of the journey was Mamre, the original point of departure. Intermediary stages were Succoth (tents) and Shechem. Mention of the former exemplifies the now familiar way of explaining the origins of a well-known locality. The latter was the necessary setting for the incident which follows and which had no original connection with the Jacob cycle.

8. Gen 34. The rape of Dinah and vengeance of Simeon and Levi

What follows is, ostensibly, the story of a *crime passionnel* and its consequences, therefore of a type quite common in the old testament (one might compare, in particular, the rape of Tamar by Amnon and the vengeance of Absalom in 2 Sam 13). Shechem son of Hamor, who belonged to a non-semitic group settled in the area, raped Dinah, the only daughter of Jacob. Afterwards, unlike Amnon and very many others, he wanted to marry her and even proposed this might be the starting point for closer relations between Shechemites and Hebrews. The latter insisted that racial intermarriage could only be contemplated on condition that the local population accepted circumcision. This stipulation was, surprisingly, accepted by Shechem and his people, little suspecting the treacherous and cowardly ruse Simeon and Levi were preparing. Then, while the male population was still recovering from this minor but painful operation, the representatives of these two tribes came on the city unawares and put all its inhabitants to the sword.

By this time we may be beginning to suspect that this kind of story featuring sexual violence, treachery and low cunning, is something of a typical product of the Hebrew imagination. Before following this up, however, we need to note once again the ability of these early writers to fictionalize the historical memories about the prehistory of Israel which had come down to them. In reality, of course, Shechem is a city, not a person, and Simeon and Levi stand for the tribes which bear their names. This short novelette is therefore concerned essentially with the violation of peaceful co-existence, confirmed by treaty and oath, between the early inhabitants of the important city of Shechem and some groups which later came to form the short-lived tribes of Simeon and Levi. These latter penetrated at an early stage into the central highlands of Palestine but were soon driven back to the south where the former merged with Judah and the latter came to have a purely cultic importance. This interpretation will be confirmed by a glance at the oracle pronounced by Jacob on these tribes (Gen 49 : 5–7).

The account of this violated treaty relationship takes us to the heart of all that we call 'religion' in the old testament. Partly because of the pejorative aura that hangs around the word 'politics', but mostly because we still tend to think of religion as a personal affair, it may be difficult to accept that in the bible the fundamental religious categories are taken from political life. Covenant means treaty, faith describes the quality of relationship between parties in a sworn treaty, sin consists in a violation of this relationship, and so on. This is not just a question of political metaphor. Neither at this time, nor for the prophets and apocalyptic writers, was a separation between politics and religion conceivable.

9. Gen 35–36. The last stage of the return. The birth of Benjamin, Esau and Edomites

The next stage of the return journey was from Shechem to Bethel. Just as the stop at Shechem was dictated by the editor's intention of inserting the tradition about the broken covenant, so the Shechem—Bethel stage seems to have been suggested by the memory of a pilgrimage or procession which used to take place ending at the latter sanctuary. Hence the renunciation and hiding of the idols, the ritual purification and change of clothes. The stop at Bethel also provided the occasion for inserting an alternative version of the changing of Jacob's name (cf 32:22–32) and the origin of the name Bethel (cf 28:10–22). It was fitting that the promise should be renewed in the most precise terms we have met so far at the religious centre which was the last visited by Jacob before his exile began twenty years earlier.

The account of the death of Rachel giving birth to Benjamin should be taken as an appendix to the earlier account of the birth of Jacob's sons (4 above). The name of ill omen ('son of my sorrow') was changed to one of good omen ('son of the right hand') though the real meaning of the name Benjamin, which is found outside the old testament, seems to be 'southerner' (the right hand indicating the south).

Benjamin is the only tribal 'hero' born in Canaan, which may indicate that this tribe came into existence in the land of Canaan. Its origins and history, at any rate, are still very obscure. Originally the southern branch of the 'Joseph tribes' (Ephraim and Manasseh), it came into prominence when Saul, a Benjaminite, became Israel's first king and fell under the lengthening shadow of Judah when Saul was eclipsed by David. At this point the grave-tradition of Rachel the tribal mother was transferred from Benjaminite to Judahite territory, ending up in Bethlehem on a site now occupied by a mosque. We need hardly be scandalized by this kind of sharp practice. It was a move dictated by political opportunism and only goes to show that in Israel as elsewhere it is usually the winning side that writes the history.

With the birth of the youngest son and the return of Jacob to his father at Hebron the Jacob cycle is complete, though he continues to feature in the long narrative about Joseph, and his death occurs only shortly before that of Joseph. Interestingly enough, we hear nothing of the death of any of the other sons.

1. How does Laban fit into the story? Does the portrayal of his character have any special significance for the writer(s)?

2. In what ways does the presentation of Jacob put the emphasis on personal growth through struggle and suffering?

3. What are the wider implications of this presentation for the existence of a christian community?

4. To what extent is the 'journey' both thematic and theologically significant in the patriarchal narratives?

5. How does the history present symbolically the themes of banishment, exile and return? How can these themes be related to the biblical meaning of salvation or redemption?

6. How do you see the relationship between the history as a whole, concerned as it is with secular realities, and the religious or cultic experiences which punctuate it? (this with special references to the theophany at Bethel, section 3).

7. How do you read the significance of the wrestling match at the Jabbok ford (section 7)?

8. In what ways do you think the idea of covenant is basic to all of these narratives, including those about Jacob?

4

The Joseph cycle
Gen 37:1–50:14

1. Gen 37:1–50:14. Joseph and his brothers

If we leave aside the interlude of chapter 38, the narrative which follows amounts to a remarkably free-flowing story, the closest we come in the old testament to the novel. Something of its spirit is captured in Thomas Mann's *Joseph and his Brothers,* though of course the Genesis story only provided him with the initial inspiration. The theme is the age-old one of triumph over misfortune; in this case, attempted murder, slavery, calumny and long imprisonment. But beneath this rags-to-riches success story there can be heard undertones which give it its own peculiar character: the note of deep moral seriousness, the passage from estrangement to reconciliation (fundamental in the scriptures), the hidden dynamic of providence. We should note in particular the function of *the dream* in taking us below the smooth surface of the narrative.

The title of the section as a whole is *The History of Jacob's Family* (37:2). Yet apart from chapter 49, which contains oracular references to the twelve tribes, the focus is on Joseph throughout. Together with Benjamin, the Joseph tribes (Ephraim and Manasseh) dominated central Palestine in early times. The story clearly reflects the ascendancy of the Joseph federation gathered around the ancient sanctuary of Shechem (for a popular explanation of this place-name see 48:22). Similarly, the role of Benjamin, the only other son of Rachel, reflects the close relationship between this tribe and its more powerful northern neighbours. Once again, therefore, we have to bear in mind the peculiar and perhaps unique way of writing history in ancient Israel.

Despite this proviso, however, the Joseph story remains one of the most remarkable and consistent pieces of fiction in early semitic literature. When we first meet him, Joseph is a rather spoilt teenager, extremely self-confident, tactless to a degree, and cordially detested by his brothers. He also has a penchant for dreaming and interpreting dreams, leading his brothers to refer to him sarcastically as 'the lord of dreams' (37:19). As soon as a favourable opportunity arose they decided to do away with him. The reader knows he will escape death—he has to since the story has hardly started—the only question is how. At this point two versions seem to have been edited in together, the one featuring Reuben and Midianite traders, the other Judah and Ishmaelites. Evidence of fine craftsmanship is the use of the long-sleeved robe as a motif. While Jacob sorrowfully looked at the bloodied garment he thought of his son in the underworld, whereas at that precise moment Joseph was beginning a new life in the household of the Egyptian chief of police.

2. Gen 38. Interlude: from the Judah cycle

The title we have given it suggests that this chapter is something of an intruder. It is in effect a small-scale cycle of narrative about Judah, the tribe which became dominant at the time of David and gave its name to judaism. The political ascendancy of this tribe, reflected in the deathbed oracle of Jacob (49:8–12) and the prophetic utterances of Balaam (Num:23–24), was only achieved after a bitter struggle which left deep resentment. Despite the political and military genius of David the union forged by him fell apart only a few decades after his death.

The story of Judah's wife and children is quite similar in several respects to the unedifying chronicles of Israel's first kings (especially the so-called 'succession history' in 2 Sam 11–1 Kgs 2). Suffice it to read the account of the rape of another Tamar by Amnon son of David, the fratricidal struggle in the latter part of David's reign, the machinations of Bathsheba (who is called Bathshua by the Chronicler). The thematic similarity is hardly coincidental.

Judah married the daughter of Shua (therefore Bathshua), a Canaanite, and had three children by her. The first two of these were killed by Yahweh under mysterious circumstances and for unspecified reasons. The second, whose name is great among the moral theologians, refused to carry out the duty of *levir* or brother-in-law, perhaps because of some grudge he bore him, and came to an untimely end. Maybe behind these goings on there lies the old folklore motif of the hexed bride, the same theme which appeared centuries later in the rather fantastic tale of Tobit—only in this case the demonic agent was the Persian devil Asmodaeus, no longer Yahweh.

The ruse of Tamar, when she realised she had been cheated by her father-in-law, was of a kind we should expect to find in the *Evergreen Press* rather than in the bible. It is narrated in a remarkably detached way free of any moralising or conclusion-drawing. Jacob had promised Tamar that she would marry his third and only surviving son, but he put her off, having evidently come to the conclusion that she was jinxed. Her plan was very simple. She dressed up as a prostitute and contrived to have intercourse with her father-in-law, thus obliging *him* to perform the levirate duty. In so doing she took the risk of shame, ostracism and violent death in her stride. The ruse paid off, she got pregnant, and the intermezzo ends with a fanciful birth-story similar to the one concerning Esau and Jacob.

From such unpromising origins as these, which any scion of a noble house today would pay a fortune to keep out of the papers, the great David issued. From such tainted origins Jesus also descended, and Tamar's name occurs in his family tree together with those of Rahab the prostitute, Ruth, another woman strong in will and execution, and the wife of the murdered Uriah.

3. Gen 39–40. Joseph's prosperity and fall from favour

The annals of the Jewish race are full of episodes like this; one of the sons of Abraham prospering in a foreign land and remaining true to the destiny and character of his people. Within this framework the writer has introduced a theme found throughout ancient and modern literature and only too familiar to cinema and TV audiences. He may have got the story of the attempted seduction and its consequences from an old Egyptian tale of two brothers one of whom is wrongly accused by the wife of the other. The tragic import of the situation may not come through strongly enough for a modern reader, though some analogy might be found, say, in Tolstoy's *Kreutzer Sonata* or Greene's *The End of the Affair*. In Israel adultery was punishable by death and in Egypt it was no light matter either, as we see from the writings of contemporary Egyptian sages. It is quite likely that Joseph lay in prison expecting to die from one day to the next.

What happened in prison is really a story within a story, following the same pattern as Joseph's fortunes on arriving in Egypt. It is even possible that the writer had in mind the old exodus motif of rescue from the land of Egypt, the house of bondage (see, for example, Deut 5:6). Joseph became the warden's man of confidence and was put in charge of two high-ranking officials who had fallen from favour. The Egyptian colouring of the story comes out clearly in the dreams of these two men which Joseph successfully interpreted. Note the grim pun about 'lifting up (off) the heads' of the troubled dreamers. As predicted, the butler got free but it was two years before he put in a word for Joseph at the court.

4. Gen 41. Return to favour. Pharaoh's dreams

This chapter is shot through with a sense of ancient piety foreign to us. The conviction that God allows foreknowledge of the future dies hard, as the growing addiction to astrology and occultism shows (it would, perhaps, be of interest to analyse our attitude to best-selling 'prophets' like Edward Cayce and Jeanne Dixon). Dreams play an important part in several patriarchal narratives generally attributed to the Elohist and, of course, in the Joseph-cycle where they generally come in pairs. After getting a bad press in the prophets—no doubt due to the exaggerated importance given them in Canaanite religion—they come back strong in the apocalyptic writers, most conspicuously in Daniel. The dreams in the Joseph-cycle have clearly influenced both jewish and christian apocalyptic circles. The vision of the heavenly woman in Rev 12, for example, takes up the symbolism of Joseph's second dream (Gen 37:9), and the dreams of Joseph husband of Mary in Mt 1–2 clearly owe much to those of his famous predecessor.

We may hear another echo of the exodus story in the contest in divination between the court magicians and Joseph. The fantastic cow-eats-cow story brought back to the mind of the butler, who was fortunately present, the dream of his unfortunate colleague about the birds eating the cakes. Joseph was summoned from prison, interpreted the dreams at once and was not only placed in charge of economic planning but made grand vizier of Egypt, second in rank only to the pharaoh himself. He at once initiated a seven-year plan designed to pull the country through the lean times ahead. As we shall learn later (47:13–26), this was to involve far-reaching social change involving something similar to a feudal order and a great increase in political centralisation. We may note in passing that this is very likely what would have happened during the Hyksos domination of Egypt (about 1720–1550 BC) with which the story of Joseph is almost certainly to be associated.

5. Gen 42–44. Joseph incognito

The theme of an incognito long maintained and at last broken, of the passage from estrangement to recognition, is full of dramatic possibilities and is used here to great effect. Will the brothers suspect? Will Joseph be able to maintain it? (Twice he had to leave their presence to hide his tears). It is difficult to avoid the conclusion that this is, basically, the work of one author who is past-master of the art of suspense.

Going beyond the merits of the narratives as such, we have to listen for the theological undertones. We are not indulging in moralising when we note the conviction underlying the story that we must pay for our moral weakness, our sins, and that the only negotiable currency is suffering. We are not talking about the so-called theory of retribution in the old testament, so profoundly criticised long afterwards in the book of Job, but of a basic moral seriousness, neglect of which leads inevitably to triviality and superficiality. We should therefore note the creative role of suffering throughout the saga cycles and especially here. This is the whole point of Joseph's testing of his brothers. In bowing down to him (42:6; 43:26) they unconsciously fulfilled his dreams and therefore (for the writer) the design of God. They were brought to the point of acknowledging the injustice of their action (42: 21–22), and it is this acknowledgment which made reconciliation possible. The anxiety, the suffering of deprivation, the repeated journeys were the means of testing the authenticity of this acknowledgement. The climax was Judah's passionate intercession for Benjamin (44:18–34) and for the old man whose life was bound up with the lad's life. After the redemptive gesture of one brother offering his life for the other, past experience had been fully purged and recognition together with reconciliation became possible.

Before passing on let us acknowledge the skill with which this story has been made to play its part in the overall context of the patriarchal history. For Israel the central historical experience was deliverance from Egypt. The Joseph cycle has the purpose of showing how Israel came to be in Egypt in the first place. We know from the history of the second millennium BC that the descent of Asiatic groups into Egypt was a common occurrence especially in times of famine. Egyptian tomb paintings represent such groups entering the country and give us some idea of what the descendants of Jacob would have looked like. The settlement of such groups in Egypt would have been greatly facilitated under the rule of the foreign Hyksos pharaohs (see the previous section) and their departure would not have been long delayed after the overthrow of these Asiatics by the pharaoh who 'knew not Joseph'. We are not therefore dealing just with a story rich in meaning. The story is a way of interpreting historical experience, of speaking to the present out of a profound meditation on the past.

6. Gen. 45. The denouement

There is little any commentator needs to add to this climax of recognition and reconciliation. Here at last the theological theme of the entire narrative about Joseph becomes explicit: behind all the evil and suffering there lies the enigma of the divine purpose. The writer does not try to explain or rationalise this enigma as we today would be tempted to do. He simply states it and leaves it at that. Later on he will speak even more clearly about God bringing good out of evil, creating new possibilities for life out of a situation which seemed desperate and intolerable (50:20). The reference to new life for a *remnant* (45:7) may be due to prophetic influence and anticipate the theology of Exodus; but the entire narrative of Genesis up to this point shows that rescue from an intolerable situation, the creation of a new possibility for life where none appeared to exist, is the characteristic act of God for these early writers.

Neither here nor later are we told why the sons of Jacob did not at once return to Canaan after the five years of famine had run their course. As has been suggested, it is probable that the settlement of these Aramaean nomads in Egypt must be associated with a definite phase in the history of the ancient Near East—the domination of the Asiatic Hyksos in Palestine and Egypt for more than a century and half. This is confirmed by the fact that they settled in the Nile Delta (where Goshen is to be located) near Joseph (45:10), that is near the capital, which was in this area only during the Hyksos period. Similarly, their bad days must have begun with the overthrow of the Hyksos (Ex 1:8ff). But, once again, we are dealing here not with history but with an attempt to interpret tradition which is a distillation of the history.

7. Gen 46:1–47:28. Jacob and his sons go down into Egypt

At the age of a hundred and thirty Jacob was called upon to make another and final journey preceded, as was the journey to Haran, by a divine revelation. In his interview with Pharaoh (47:7–10) Jacob said, in effect, that his whole life had been that of a man on the move, an alien in foreign lands who had never been allowed to settle in. This emphasis on sojourning is perhaps the basic theological theme of the patriarchal narratives. It indicates a life oriented at every stage towards a future fulfilment, the acceptance of present insecurity in view of a future in which one will not share personally but in the creation of which one is called to participate. When we as christians speak of 'hope' we should bear in mind the experience of men like Jacob.

The assurance given Jacob that he will return obviously does not refer to the bringing back of his corpse and its burial in the land of Canaan. He will return not in his own person but in the corporate personality of the community which, many years later, will take possession of the land. This way of thinking, which gives such little importance to personal survival and implies so high a degree of identification with the destiny of a group, has been undermined by the whole trend of philosophical and religious thinking in the West. In the old testament the theme of an ongoing promise cannot be understood apart from this idea of 'corporate personality'; though we may have to re-interpret and re-express the meaning of this latter we cannot think of it as simply archaic, a category peculiar to a primitive and tribal way of life. Today, more than ever before, we are being called out into a consciousness of the entire community of mankind.

The priestly editors have inserted at this point a list of the descendants of Israel (Jacob). They have drawn it up to tally with the fixed traditional figure of seventy (see Ex 1:5; Deut 10:22) which of course is the 'sacred number' multiplied by ten. Maybe Luke had this in mind when he added the section, peculiar to his gospel, of the sending out of the seventy disciples in addition to the Twelve (10:1); though we should recall that in Jewish tradition the number of the nations is also seventy.

After the highly emotional meeting between Jacob and Joseph, reunited after twenty-two years, arrangements were made for re-settlement in Egypt. The note about shepherds being an abomination to the Egyptians tallies well with what we know of Egyptian national pride and a marked tendency to xenophobia. Jacob's audience with Pharaoh rings true enough, though we may doubt whether he would have blessed the divine monarch, source of life, blessing and every good to his subjects. The final passage, which deals with Joseph's agrarian policy, has often provided ammunition for anti-semitic propaganda though, as is usually true of this kind of loaded treatment of texts, no case can be made out. Increasing centralization and taxation on property did indeed take place in Egyptian history but it would be naive to trace it back to Joseph. Essentially all the writer wishes to say is that, by whatever means, Joseph saved Egypt from a great and imminent catastrophe.

8. Gen 47:29–50:26. Last dispositions and death of Jacob. Death of Joseph

We are now approaching the end of this long history. Jacob made Joseph swear a solemn oath to bury him in Canaan, a charge which is repeated after the deathbed oracles (49:29–32). As with Abraham, this was in view of a future fulfilment, a last declaration of faith in a future where God was waiting for his people. It should be obvious by now that this orientation towards the future underlies not only these narratives but the entire biblical record. We might compare with this last disposition of Jacob the experience of Jeremiah who also died in Egypt but not before buying a plot of land in the doomed kingdom of Judah. By their insistence, both Abraham and Jacob staked a claim in the future for the community which was still to come into existence.

Passing on for the moment to the last chapter, we might note how two irreconcilable traditions about where Jacob was buried have been conflated together. According to one he was embalmed and given the full rites of mourning normally reserved to a king (seventy-two days in Egypt). He was then buried somewhere east of the Jordan in a tomb prepared by himself (not by Abraham) at a place for which the usual popular explanation is given (Abel-misraim = Egyptian mourning). According

to the other, which has become normative, he was buried
with his forefathers in the cave bought by Abraham.
These two traditions have been rolled into one by a
journey to Hebron involving a quite unnecessary detour
through Transjordan.

The reader will by now suspect that there is more to
the blessing of Joseph's sons than a simple incident in a
story. Jacob took them on his knees, a gesture indicating
acceptance or adoption widespread in the ancient Semitic
East, and then conferred on them his penultimate blessing. The incident of the crossing of the arms can only be
understood in the light of the history of these two tribes.
The political predominance of Manasseh passed at an
early stage to Ephraim following on which Shechem,
which was in Manasseh and upon which a popular etymology is conferred here, lost its pre-eminence as a religious centre to Shiloh in Ephraim. The importance of
these two centrally located tribes is further emphasised in
the deathbed oracle which follows (49 : 22–26). Much of
the material in this chapter is only ostensibly prophetic;
indications abound that the sayings on the tribes come
from a time several centuries after the patriarchal age.
The Judah oracle, which has played such an important
part in Jewish and christian tradition, seems to suggest
the early part of David's reign as the time of composition.
This, however, would not necessarily be the case for all
the sayings.

The narrative-cycle had begun with Joseph's dream,
the hatred it aroused in his brothers and the attempted
murder which followed. The climax now comes when the
same brothers fall down before him (50 : 18), as had been
foretold, but the deeper meaning of the events is unfolded
in Joseph's answer to their unspoken plea for forgiveness.
The originality of the idea of 'good out of evil' may easily

be missed it is by no means self-evident that good can flow from evil intent. Joseph is speaking of two levels of intentionality: '*you* meant evil against me, but *God* meant it for good'. Here we have, from the prophetic Elohist source, the profoundly original idea that even the consequences of bad will and moral weakness can be caught up and transformed in the divine plan. Once the brothers come to recognise and acknowledge this, forgiveness and reconciliation can follow. Many people are kept alive (rescued from death), the future remains open and the stage is set for the next scene of the drama.

1. What do you take to be the dominant theme of the Joseph cycle? What is its function in the wider context of the history of the people?

2. Comment, with reference to the Onan episode (section 2), on the effects of biblical (mis)interpretation on sexual attitudes current among many christians today.

3. Granted the importance within the narrative of the moment of recognition and reconciliation, what are its wider, theological implications?

4. How can the idea of 'corporate personality' be restated today?

5. Could the patriarchal narratives as a whole serve as a basis for stronger and more persuasive theology of hope than those we have been accustomed to?

Exodus

John Challenor

Introduction

The OT scriptures, which came into being during a period of nearly a thousand years, are built up on the Exodus event, like coral. Coral is a hard growth built up from the skeletons of minute creatures called polyps which keep on being added to a small original nucleus. So that eventually a whole island, or a reef a thousand miles long, can be the outcome.

The nucleus of the OT was the exodus event. The first celebration of the event that we can discern was by Miriam and her dancing girls (Ex 15 : 21). As they danced, they told the story, and were no doubt encouraged by the men of Israel to repeat the performance. A ritual was born. The historical books of the OT are written around this event, carrying the story of God's dealings with his people forward, and (in Genesis) backward. The prophets recall Israel to faith in Yahweh 'who brought you up out of the land of Egypt.' The wisdom books outline in a new and more worldly idiom the good life that the Sinai law prescribes.

To open the OT scriptures at random can be like being lost without a landmark among the meandering channels of the Nile delta. But just as every channel can be followed upstream to the main river and to its source, so every verse of the OT can be referred eventually to its one source in the revelation of the old covenant, even to Ex

14:21–22, where Israel escaped from the Egyptian army at the sea by night.

When christians meet to celebrate the death and resurrection of Christ and eat the meal of the new covenant, they recall the old covenant and Israel's exodus. The new covenant did not destroy the old when it superseded it. Marcion, in the second century, wanted the church to disown the OT scriptures, and his error led us to affirm our full acceptance of them as the record of God's doings and his people's response, prior to Christ. The OT was scripture for the early church: when the NT emerges, it shows clearly that the church interpreted the phenomenon of Christ in terms of the OT. As the two disciples walked towards Emmaüs, discussing the puzzling events of the previous few days in Jerusalem, a stranger explained these events to them with reference to Moses and the prophets and the scriptures they thought they understood (Lk 24:27). In reading the OT scriptures, and in discussing and examining their meaning, we are at one with the first followers of the Lord, and in his risen presence.

This outline is not intended as something to be read for its own sake. It has the modest aim of facilitating much more important doings—the study of Exodus itself; the discussion of its meaning for us today, through the questions at the end of each section, and others; and the study of theology in general, which has for too long been unduly specialised, and mistakenly reckoned as beyond the powers of all but a few in the church.

Book list

Some of the books drawn upon in this outline, and recommended for further study:

The Jerusalem Bible, for its text, notes and index of theological themes.

M. Noth, *Exodus*. The best commentary.

R. de Vaux, *Ancient Israel*. An encyclopaedic work.

G. von Rad, *Old Testament Theology*. Profound and very influential.

John Bright, *A History of Israel*.

B. W. Anderson, *The Living World of the Old Testament*. A very readable general introduction.

G. E. Wright and R. Fuller, *The Book of the Acts of God*. Another fine introduction to scripture, in the Penguin series.

Thierry Maertens, *A Feast in Honour of Yahweh*. A study of OT worship.

J. J. Stamm and M. E. Andrew, *The Ten Commandments in Recent Research*.

H. Frankfort (ed), *Before Philosophy*. On the myths and thought-forms of ancient Egypt (Penguin).

D. Daube, *The Exodus Pattern in the Bible*.

1

Exodus: the background

The RSV gives the book the careful title, 'the second book of Moses, commonly called Exodus', and we who in our common way speak of Exodus as if it were a separate work are reminded that it is really part two of a five-volume work, the Pentateuch. Part one, Genesis, ends by telling us how the twelve sons of Jacob (whose other name, Israel, was passed on to the whole people after him) came to be in Egypt. And the remaining three parts, Leviticus, Numbers, and Deuteronomy, continue the story of Israel, their law, their worship, and their various adventures, as they journey on towards the land of Canaan. One interesting short introduction to Exodus, seen through christian eyes (and slanted for particular polemical purposes) is Acts 7—the speech made by Stephen which cost him his life.

But in one way Exodus is the first book and the foundation of the OT, in that it relates how Israel first came to exist as a people conscious of their identity, and consequently interested in preserving the traditions about their ancestors, and in joining their story to the early history of God's dealings with mankind as a whole. These traditions are found in Genesis, which some say is like a preface, written last, after the main work, to help the reader look in the right direction.

The word 'exodus'—the going forth out (of Egypt)—
is the Latin form of a similar Greek word found in the
Greek translation of the OT at Ex 19:1. The exodus event,
which is pin-pointed at Ex 14:21–22, was understood as
a rescue from slavery into freedom in the possession of
Yahweh, and as the preliminary to settlement in the land
of Canaan. As such it had, and has, for Israel something
of the value and importance the Great Trek can have for
the Afrikaner, the Long March for the Chinese commu-
nist, the voyage of the *Mayflower* for the US citizen, and
the withdrawal of an occupying power for the people of
some colonial or conquered territory.

At the time of the exodus, there were in the near east
broadly two sorts of people. There were the settled agrarian cultivators, or sedentary crop-raisers, living relatively
prosperously in larger political units. And there were the
wandering pastoral tribesmen, or nomadic herd-raisers,
living in relative poverty in smaller clan and family units.
The story in Gen 4 of Cain, a tiller of the ground, and
Abel, a keeper of sheep, makes the distinction, and illustrates the hostility between the two groups.

The fertile parts, Egypt and Canaan, contained cultivators. The drier land between and around Egypt and
Canaan—the Sinai peninsula in particular—was occupied by nomads who moved continually on in search of
water and fresh pasture for their animals. The nomadic
family of Jacob had been forced by drought and famine
to seek food in Egypt. Unusually favoured at first, they
settled as free men on the edge of the cultivated area of
the Nile delta. Later they were turned into slave labourers and used as construction workers. At the exodus, they
resumed their nomadic wanderings for a time, until they
invaded Canaan and settled there as cultivators—of 'corn,
and wine, and oil'.

Egypt, like China, where the economy was similarly built upon a great river or rivers, early developed a centralised imperial government. This answered the need to try to regulate the river's flow, to organise relief in time of drought and to build defences in time of flood—and to do this in a co-ordinated way for a large area. But with central control came the possibilities of organised governmental oppression, and of political stagnation and immobilism.

John Wilson in *Before Philosophy* describes ancient Egypt as 'a green gash of teeming life cutting across brown desert wastes'. A clear line divides life from non-life. There is no rain. Life comes from the sun, and from the Nile. Together, in normal years, these gave Egypt two good crops, one early and one late, so that 'corn in Egypt' became a name for plenty. Of the sun and the Nile, the sun was the more regular. So the personification of the sun was the supreme creator-god, Re, who every night overcame the hostile snake Apophis, the power of darkness, and every morning rose victorious from the underworld.

The Nile had a corresponding, but annual, cycle of birth and death. At one season, the river lies quiet and slow between shrunken banks, while what were fields beside it turn to dust, and the desert closes in. Then as life ebbs away, the Nile stirs again with a pulse of power. Far away to the south, many weeks before, heavy rain has fallen. The Nile swells and swirls and races, and then overflows its banks and floods the flat land for miles on either side. (Herodotus noted that the flood reached in some places for two days' journey from the main stream.) When the flood subsides, it leaves fertile mud behind. A frenzied sowing, and soon a broad green carpet of growing fields completes the annual wonder of the victory of life over death. Most years, this happened. But some years, when rainfall was low, the river failed to perform its duty, and there was famine.

Pharaoh (like 'caesar' a title, not a name), himself one of the gods, was responsible for bringing forth the waters of life for his people. He performed the ritual magic observances to help on the due working of the seasonal cycle. The pharaohs also performed the difficult task of holding together upper and lower Egypt—virtually two distinct entities, apart from their common dependence on the Nile—and made Egypt a strong and unusually stable power. But government was paternalistic. Pharaoh was proprietor of all the land (Gen 47:20). He was himself subject to a suffocating routine of protocol and precedent. All Egypt was much obsessed by death—her burial customs earned her the nickname 'death' in the ancient world. Some of this contempt seems to be reflected in the feelings of Israel towards Egypt as conveyed in Ex 1–15.

A reason for mentioning Egypt in some detail is that its routine 'nature-religion' provides a contrast with Israel's dynamic 'religion of history'. Israel encountered another nature-religion, discordant with her own, when she settled in Canaan. Unlike Egypt, Canaan was a land of small city-states, which practised a worship of local deities (Baals), with the object of helping on the working of the seasonal cycle and so promoting the fertility of the land. Exodus, edited as it was after the occupation of Canaan, shows traces of Israel's abhorrence of Baal-worship (Ex 34:13).

About 1220 BC Pharaoh Merneptah suppressed a rising in Canaan and left us the only reference to Israel that exists in Egyptian sources. On the back of a stone slab of black granite set up by an earlier pharaoh, he had the story of his conquests inscribed. The reference to Israel reads: 'Israel lies desolate; her seed is no more . . . everyone who was a nomad has been curbed by King Merneptah.'

So some at least of the tribes were in Canaan by 1220. This suggests that the exodus was before 1250, which would put it in the reign of Rameses II, a great builder who moved the capital from Thebes down to the delta, and who fits the description of the pharaoh given in Exodus.

Diggings on the east side of the Jordan suggest that until 1300 there were only roaming Beduin tribes there; whereas after 1300 there grew up settled kingdoms with fortifications—Edom and Moab. Since 20:14 presents Israel asking Edom for right of passage on her way to Canaan, it seems that the exodus could not have been earlier than 1300. So though the evidence is rather fragmentary and uncertain, most people now assume the exodus took place between 1300 and 1250.

But Exodus is not a straightforward piece of history, and was not written by any one author. Like the rest of the Pentateuch, it is a compilation by later editors of early material that was passed on orally in Israel, especially in gatherings for worship. The attentive reader will find discrepancies, duplications and differences of style and point of view.

For example Ex 3:15 and 6:3 seem to represent different traditions. One, set in Sinai, tells us that Israel's ancestors (Abraham and Isaac) had always known God as Yahweh; the other, set in Egypt, says that God revealed his name Yahweh for the first time to Moses. Again Ex 24 seems to recount two different covenant ceremonies, presenting them as one; if we try to visualise one ceremony, we are left with an irremediably blurred picture.

Again the narrative style of the opening chapters is very

different from that of the rules for worship in chapters
25–31, which the modern reader is tempted to skip as
small print, and which in all their elaboration can hardly
belong to Israel's nomadic period before entering Canaan.

The working hypothesis adopted by most scholars today to account for the lack of unity in Exodus is, briefly,
as follows. In the ninth century, when Israel was settled
in Jerusalem, a writer we call 'J' (because he considers
Israel knew God from the beginning as Yahweh—
Jahweh) edited the basic story. Into this, soon after, was
worked another version of Israel's traditions, edited by a
writer 'E' who uses the term Elohim, not the name Yahweh, for God. Later, about the sixth century, 'P' the
priestly school of writers, re-edited the story, adding other
material, some of it reflecting the point of view of established temple worship in Jerusalem, and including the
assertion that God revealed his name Yahweh for the first
time to Moses. Judging from the names given to children, as discovered from archaeological research, and from
the worship of Abraham, Isaac, and Jacob as glimpsed in
Genesis, P was historically right on this point. This warns
us that though P wrote late, that school preserved oral
material much of which was of great historical reliability.

How accurate and reliable, historically, is the book as a
whole? There are two extreme views, between which the
truth fairly certainly lies. One is that thanks to divine
inspiration and the care with which the oral traditions
were handed on, the story tells us exactly what actually
happened. The other is that the exodus was part of
Israel's prehistory, and that the story as we have it is a
reconstruction, a backward projection from a later stand-
point when Israel was settled in Canaan and in a position
to set in order her traditions of the past. (In one version
of this view, Moses is like King Arthur, a figure of legend

rather than history.) What view the reader takes is for him or her to decide.

Meanwhile this outline will assume that except where there is evidence to the contrary, the story is substantially faithful to the facts, but with the proviso that it would be anachronistic of us if we hoped to find in the OT our modern interest in 'what actually happened,' as distinct from received accounts and traditional interpretations. The OT narratives were not recited and remembered for the sake of the historical information they contain, but because of their importance as the material of worship and the means of ordering community life. In other words Exodus is not, by our standards, a history book. Israel called it a book of the law. We might translate that best by calling it a book of theology—in the deepest sense—a book about the call of God, and man's response of faith.

1. What were the two main types of social organisation in the near east around 1250 BC? Is there any comparable differentiation in the world today?

2. What is a nature-religion?

3. On the matter of the knowledge of God's name, could Ex 3 (JE) be historically wrong but theologically right?

4. Are there traces of antisemitism in Acts 7?

2

Slaves in Egypt
Ex 1:1–7:7

Ex 1

Joseph had been prime minister of Egypt (Gen 41) and had drawn his family to settle there, in the north-east, on the side of the delta nearest to Sinai. The period of official favour passed. A later pharaoh feared the growing clan of immigrants, who might align themselves with other nomadic invaders and disturb the peace of Egypt. A policy of suppression was decided on. The immigrants were reduced to the status of slave-labourers, and some rudimentary measures of population control were attempted.

It is possible that several hundred years separated Jacob from Moses. Ex 12:40 calls it four hundred and thirty, and Paul repeats this in Gal 3:17. But Ex 6:14 counts only four generations—perhaps a century—from Jacob to Moses.

It is also possible that some of the twelve tribes were never in Egypt, but migrated from Sinai straight into Canaan, joining the tribes from Egypt at Shechem, at such a ceremony as that recounted in Josh 24. (More on this in the next section, at 12:38.) They were after all still nomads, and P (who wrote the introductory verses 1–7) may be schematising and back-dating the later twelve-tribe confederacy. His purpose in listing the tribal

founders and noting the great increase in Israel's population is probably to indicate that God was looking after
his people.

The term 'Hebrew' is used for Israel in the early part
of Exodus. Near-Eastern records of the second millennium BC speak quite often of 'Habiru', probably the same
term. These Habiru seem to have been, not any particular
ethnic group, but a large social class all over the Near
East—propertyless nomads attracted to the urban settlements, and being reported either as lawless raiders or as
enslaved labourers. Probably Egypt classified Israel as belonging to this category of people.

Ex 2

Perhaps to forestall an awkward question, the story goes
on to account for the strange circumstance that Moses, the
Israelite par excellence, was brought up as an Egyptian.
Nursed by his own mother, he could be accepted as an
Israelite adopted by Pharaoh's daughter, he was also 'in-
structed in all the wisdom of the Egyptians' (Acts 7: 22).
The name Moses, like Rameses and Thutmose, is Egyptian—the etymology in 2:10 is rather patriotic than fact-
ual. Pharaoh's daughter would hardly know Hebrew.

Solidarity with his own people leads Moses to kill an
Egyptian. The Israelites, so far from being ripe for revolt,
exhibit a slave mentality (2:14; see also 5:21 and 6:9).
Moses leaves the country, and settles with Midianites,
camel-nomads who roamed in Sinai and the Arabian
desert. He works for the Midianite priest Reuel (called
Jethro in another tradition at 18:1) and marries one of
his daughters. While Moses is abroad, the Lord himself
intervenes.

Ex 3

At the mountain of God, Horeb (probably Mount Sinai under a different name) Moses is called, given a revelation of God—or is it a revelation of God's plan?—and commissioned to bring Israel out of Egypt.

Ex 3:14, and the whole problem of the name of God, have proved difficult. The older English bibles used 'the LORD' to translate the Hebrew YHWH. From the thirteenth century AD, this Hebrew name was mistakenly reconstructed as 'Jehovah'. The mistake was possible because Hebrew was written orginally without vowels, and because out of reverence the holy name gradually ceased after 300 BC to be pronounced out loud. In reading, the word Adonai (Lord) was substituted, and in writing, the vowels of Adonai were added to the consonants of YHWH —whence the mistaken 'Jehovah'. It is thought now that the name of God was originally pronounced 'Yahweh', a form connected with the verb 'to be', so as to have a sound like 'he is', or 'he will be'.

The Greek translation of the OT rendered the central part of 3:14 'I am he who is', using the present participle of the verb 'to be', as if to say 'I am the being one'. On this translation much traditional theology built up an idea of God as he who in the most fundamental way, really exists— he who gives derived being to all created things—the eternal, changeless one who alone possesses the quality of 'aseity' or independent being. This is all very well once Greek philosophy, in particular ontology, comes along, five hundred to a thousand years after Moses. But many scholars today deny that Israel could have understood 'Yahweh' in this abstract way, since they had not the Greek philosophical mentality, nor the corresponding language to do so.

Another possibility is that 'I am who I am' is

deliberately enigmatic—God's refusal to disclose himself clearly, as a parent might tell an importunate child to wait and see. Into the obscurity of this mysterious formula (which, as the footnotes show, we do not even know how to translate!), God withdraws himself so that Israel cannot presume to conjure up his power, or use or exploit him for her own purposes. Yahweh is *free* (Ex 33:19).

I. T. Ramsey suggests that what 3:14 gives us is, not a name at all, but a tautology—'I am I'—an inexplicable ultimate option, like the one a man might use to express his commitment to his wife: he might say, if pressed repeatedly to explain why he loves her, 'because she is who she is'. The irreducible elusiveness of the divine name is a necessary safeguard to prevent us worshipping—idolatrously—a name or a mental image instead of God himself. To confirm this explanation, its supporters point to what they claim is a similar prohibition—the veto on carved images (Ex 20:7).

But even this solution leaves others unconvinced. If, they argue, what happened at the burning bush was not a disclosure of information about God's being and nature, neither was it a non-disclosure, a withholding of information. In talking of information, something within our reach for the mind to possess, whether positively or negatively, we are (they say) using the wrong category. Moses, and Israel, would have understood what happened at the burning bush as a promise of God's effective presence and future saving action. In simple terms, (they suggest), Moses understood God to say, 'I am with you'. Or, since Buber and von Rad prefer the translation 'I will be who I will be', then, 'I will be with you'.

We should read Exodus through before attempting to decide the matter. Significantly, the OT never again speaks of God as 'I am who I am', nor again concerns itself with the derivation of Yahweh's name. But it does repeatedly speak of Yahweh as 'he who brought up his people out of Egypt with a mighty hand'. The description of Yahweh in Ex 34 : 6–7, as known *in relation to Israel* is more characteristic of the OT. In other words, what seems to have come to Moses was an assurance of Yahweh's relationship to Israel. As Israel is the people of Yahweh, Yahweh is the God of Israel. (It is worth looking up what Christ said about the happening at the burning bush, Mk 12 : 26.)

J-B Metz (in *The Word in History*, pp 75-6) writes as follows

> Recent exegetical researches indicate that the words of revelation in the OT are not primarily words of statement or of information, nor are they mainly words of appeal or of personal self-communication by God, but they are words of promise. Their statement is announcement, their announcement is proclamation of what is to come, and therefore the abrogation of what is . . . God reveals himself to Moses more as the power of the future than as a being dwelling beyond all history and experience. God is not 'above us' but 'before us'. His transcendence reveals itself as our 'absolute future'.

Exodus makes rather a point of the despoiling of the Egyptians. The instructions about it occur at 3 : 21 and again at 11 : 2. The thing is done at 12 : 35. Daube suggests that the later Israelite procedure for the freeing of slaves has been projected back into the exodus story. Deut 15 : 12–15 lays down that a slave, on being freed, must be furnished generously with possessions. Others think that what is said to have happened, happened. In either case, the story adds to the spirit of jubilation.

Ex 4

To Moses, who is diffident about his capacity to persuade Israel, God gives some wonder-working powers, and the help of Aaron as spokesman. On the way back to Egypt, a mysterious episode is recorded (4:24)—possibly a local demon story, rewritten to concord with the Yahweh faith, and used as an occasion for teaching the importance of circumcision. (The story may have affinities with the story of Jacob wrestling with an angel, in Gen 32.)

Ex 5–7

In 6:2–13 is another account (P) of Moses' call, additional to the JE account in Ex 3. Here the scene is Egypt. The author is explicit that the name Yahweh is only now revealed. The covenant is looked on as already established, with Abraham (Gen 15:16), and even with Noah (Gen 9:9). For JE on the other hand, the covenant is only now in process of being made.

1. What difficulties did Moses have in rousing Israel to revolt and escape?

2. Is it possible to interpret the words of Yahweh at the burning bush as primarily a record of the call of Moses, like the calls of other prophets (Is 6:1, Jer 1:4)?

3. In 1654, Pascal experienced a 'second conversion', when he discovered 'the God of Abraham, and the God of Isaac, and the God of Jacob, and not of the philosophers and the scientists.' He carried the account of this experience, sewn in his clothes, for the rest of his life. What does his discovery mean to you?

4. What do you understand by the 'transcendence' of God, as illustrated in these stories?

3

Escape
Ex 7:8-15:21

Ex 7:8-10:29. The first nine plagues

These products of the ancient storytellers' art may seem
tediously repetitive today. Incidents similar in structure
follow one after another. In many cases, the story is told
twice, once as destined to happen, and then all over again
as having happened. The impression is given (7:25) that
when one plague was over, the next broke out within the
week. And yet if all the Egyptian livestock died of plague
(9:6), it is hard to see how boils (9:10) or hail (9:25)
could be any further worry to them. . . But of course this
is too literal-minded an approach, the wrong level at
which to read the story. The narrators' overriding purpose is to glorify Yahweh and to celebrate his victory over
the stupid pharaoh who made himself ridiculous by ob-
stinately backing the losing side. In Israel's early days the
stories aroused jubilation and faith and worship; the
hearers would savour the delicious long-drawn-out suspense before the final happy ending.

The question arises, were these miraculous happenings? People tend to give one of three answers. (1) The
plagues were miracles. The inspired narrative is clear :
Yahweh was at work. If we doubt the miraculous here,
where do we end? What becomes of Jesus's resurrection?
(2) We no longer believe in any miraculous element in

the plagues. All were more or less familiar natural phenomena in Egypt. In Pharaoh's magicians turning their
rods into serpents, we have an obvious example of folklore and legend. It is simply that the plague stories have
grown in the telling. (3) The plagues were 'signs and
wonders' (7:3). The Egyptians are annoyed, but see
nothing entirely out of the ordinary, until perhaps after
the tenth plague, when Pharaoh asks for Moses's intercession. Israel's leaders, on the other hand, become con-
vinced that Yahweh is intervening on their behalf. For
Israel, as for the rest of the ancient world, there was not
the clear discontinuity between the natural and the miraculous, the ordinary and the extraordinary, which became
part of modern Europe's mental outlook with Isaac New-
ton. Any everyday event could be a sign to Israel of Yahweh's activity. Surely the final outcome, the very existence of Israel, is sufficient to convince the eye of faith
that Yahweh was fighting for Israel? Israel might have
said, appealing to the data of experience: 'One thing we
know; we were slaves in Egypt, and now we are free' (cf
Jn 9:25).

Ex 11:1–13:16. Plague ten and the passover

The warning about the last plague occupies 11. The
plague, and Israel's departure, are narrated in 12:29–39.
All the rest of this section is instruction about the carrying out of the passover liturgy. In this way, the passover,
as celebrated in Israel after the settlement in Canaan, was
linked with their immunity from the last plague, and
with the exodus. Of the two cultures of the time, nomadic
and agrarian, each had its characteristic spring festival.
The nomads sacrificed an animal from the herd; the agra-
rians offered a sheaf from the crop. The nomads, before

their annual exodus to new spring pastures, would kill a lamb and daub its blood at the tent-door as a protection against evil spirits; the cultivators would bring the first-fruits of the early harvest in thanksgiving. In particular, at the spring new year, the cultivators would eat their bread unleavened ('azyme', without yeast) in order to avoid 'mixing the spirits'—mixing this year's flour with yeast made from last year's flour. They waited some days until they had yeast made from this year's crop.

Here then are two quite separate observances. After settling in Canaan, Israel adopted the agrarian feast, and added it to her own nomadic feast. The two more or less fused. The passion narrative speaks of the two as connected, though distinct (Mk 14 : 1), and as identical (Lk 22 : 1). The passover lamb celebration—a single evening meal—was followed by seven days of unleavened bread. The latest editors of Ex 12–13 lived at a time when Israel was in a position to impose slavery on others (Ex 12 : 43–49). Israel attributes the feasts, and their linking, to the exodus event and the will of Yahweh. The general nomadic lamb-offering was transformed into an offering to Yahweh; the action of the evil spirits of the pagans was ascribed to the Lord himself, or to his destroying angel, who slew the Egyptian first-born, but passed over the houses of Israel. And Israel assimilated the old custom of the unleavened bread by detaching it from its original context in a religion of nature, and inserting it into their own religion of history. It was attached to the exodus event with a historical explanation—that the people left Egypt in such haste that there was no time to leaven the dough and wait for it to rise (Ex 12 : 34, 39).

The basic religious education of children is ensured in Ex 12 : 26–27 and 13 : 7–8, which give rise to an explanatory catechetical dialogue whenever a Jewish family keeps the passover. 'Why is this night different from other nights?', the youngest child is briefed to ask—and some other questions. The father of the family answers by reading part of the passover story.

Ex 13 loosely connects the custom of offering Israelite first-born to God with the sparing of them in the last plague. Note that Christ's presentation and redemption (Lk 2 : 22) is recounted in terms of Ex 13.

The figure of 600,000 men is not historically realistic. It probably comes from adding together the numerical values of the Hebrew consonants in the words 'sons of Israel'. Pharaoh's army at full strength numbered only 20,000; and Israel was not numerous enough to take Canaan all at once (Ex 23 : 30, and Jgs 1 : 1). But that those who escaped were a 'mixed crowd' (12 : 38) does seem to be accurate. Despite Ex 1 : 1–4, there is evidence to suggest that some of the twelve tribes were never in Egypt, but emigrated from Sinai into Canaan independently. The covenant renewal ceremony in Josh 24 suggests the inclusion of converts into the twelve-tribe confederacy. The absence of any record in the conquest stories of the taking of Shechem and central Palestine indicated that it was already in friendly hands. And it is extremely likely that other slave-labourers in Egypt, unconnected with Jacob by blood, joined Israel and escaped with them.

Ex 13:17–15:21. The wonder at 'the sea'

As far as Pharaoh was concerned, the people of Israel were going a three-day journey towards Sinai, to worship their God. After the climax of the tenth plague, a further climax follows—Pharaoh's pursuit is thwarted by Yahweh.

Israel avoided the highway to Canaan along the Mediterranean coast, which was used by the military and commercial establishment. (It was not yet 'the way of the land of the Philistines': these did not arrive till the twelfth century, after the exodus. Again, evidence of later editing.) Israel made for the desert of Sinai, by way of the isthmus where the Suez Canal now runs. They made for what the Hebrew calls *yam suph*, the sea of reeds or lake of papyrus (13:18) which no one has exactly located, but which was probably a marshy area between Lake Timsah and the Bitter Lakes, or between the Bitter Lakes and the Gulf of Suez. The Red Sea is far to the south. Hebrew has only the one word *yam* for sea and lake, and the translators who put the Hebrew into Greek seem to have made a guess at the botanical word *suph* and rendered it 'red'. The idea that Israel crossed the Red Sea passed from the Greek Septuagint into the Latin Vulgate and thence into almost all the versions until quite recently.

Ex 14

After a long discussion on the actual exodus event—the escape from pursuit—Martin Noth concludes, 'This fact of the saving of Israel through the destruction of an Egyptian chariot force in "the sea" forms the historical basis of the tradition'. It is impossible now to reconstruct the event in detail. The narrators' object is still to glorify Yahweh. Israel, at the critical juncture, is presented as otherwise defenceless. (But 'Fear not', says Moses. The incident in the boat on the lake during the storm—Mk 4:35–41, and the separation of water and dry land—Gen 1:1–10, both deserve to be referred to at this point.)

Yahweh saved Israel (14:30); redeemed her (15:13); purchased her (15:16), he was her salvation (15:2).

The picture of the waters rising like walls to right and left (14:22) is from P. It is probably an embellishment, comparable to the further poetic treatment of the event in the Psalms (Ps 78:13; Ps 106; Ps 114).

Ex 15

Ex 15:20–21 is probably a very early liturgical song—possibly the first portion of the OT to be articulated. It contains the basic twofold structure of liturgy—a call to praise God, and a mention of the reason for doing so. (This is the structure of any eucharistic preface, and of the Easter vigil proclamation, the *Exsultet.*) 15:1–18 is a longer song on the same theme, presumably later, since 15:17 suggests that Jerusalem is in Israelite hands, which it was only with David, after 1000 BC.

1. Who is the hero of the story so far? Moses? Aaron? Israel as a whole? If not, who? What does the answer suggest about the literary genre or category that Exodus belongs to?

2. The exodus story is loaded with extraordinary happenings. How are these to be understood today?

3. If the Egyptian government had recorded Israel's departure, how might they have done it? Does this throw any light on the nature of divine revelation?

4. What is to be thought of Israel's primitive method of religious education—the catechetical method in a family liturgical setting?

5. Harvey Cox (in The Secular City) claims that by the exodus revolt Yahweh freed Israel, and us, from belief in divine right of kings and governments; taught us not to accept uncritically any socio-political order; and set us in a revolutionary tradition of dissatisfaction with every successive status quo. Is this a reasonable claim?

6. Do the events of this section throw any light on what happened at the burning bush?

7. How far does it seem that Israel understood their salvation in terms of this world—political independence and freedom of worship; and how far in terms of another world—in 'spiritual' or 'supernatural' terms?

4

The journey onward to Sinai
Ex 15:22–18:27

Once free—and unprovided for by the Egyptian government—Israel had to face the tasks of finding food and drink, defending themselves, and organising their social life. Roughly, chapters 16, 17 and 18 indicate what was done in these three areas.

Ex 15:22–17:7. Food and drink

Moses perhaps knew of some herb which made water more drinkable. The manna is produced by insects which suck at tamarisk bushes and secrete a sweet substance on leaves and branches overnight, which ants eat during the day. Quails migrate in flocks in spring, and can be trapped fairly easily. The story of the manna conveys a lesson on God's providential care of his people, and another about keeping the sabbath rest. The mention of the sabbath at 16:23 is the earliest—it comes even before the law about it is given at Sinai (20:8). Astrologers in ancient Sumer and Babylon declared certain days, including the seventh of every lunar cycle, unlucky. To work was to incur divine displeasure, so a rest was established, which no doubt became a popular institution for its own sake. Maertens and others hold that Israel accepted this social custom, providing the quite different explanation that Yahweh's six-day work of creation was followed by a sabbath rest (Gen 2 : 1–3; Ex 20 : 11).

The authors envisage a pot of manna set beside the ark of the covenant as a memorial of God's providence in the desert. Nothing is known from other sources of any such pot. If there was one, it may have been lost when the Philistines captured the ark about 1050 BC (1 Sam 4).

Looking behind the immediate events, it seems that the narrators stress the conflict of faith and doubt that went on. 'Is the Lord among us, or not?' the people ask (17 : 7). They grumble against Moses; they accuse him of bringing them into the desert to kill them with hunger and thirst; and they paint a glowing picture of the life of plenty they enjoyed in Egypt. It is vividly expressed in Num 11 : 4–6 (where, however, some attempt is made to present the grumbling as coming not from the people as a whole, but from a section only)

> Now the rabble that was among them had a strong craving; and the people of Israel also wept again, and said, 'O that we had meat to eat! We remember the fish we ate in Egypt for nothing, the cucumbers, the melons, the leeks, the onions, and the garlic; but now our strength is dried up, and there is nothing at all but this manna to look at. (See also Num 20 : 5.)

There was even a possibility of violence against Moses (Ex 17 : 4). It seems that the people directed towards Moses, 'for forty years', much of the hatred they felt for Yahweh (mixed with their love) because he had led them away from security and was making unlimited demands on them. What faith in Yahweh meant for Israel, we can understand more clearly if we notice what counted as the opposite of faith. It seems that faithlessness meant, not modern unbelief, or doubt about his existence, but rather a lack of trust in Yahweh's unwavering steadfast reliability; and practical preference for other means of security.

Ex 17:8–16. Defence

Amalek was a rival nomadic people who no doubt resented Israel as trespassers in Sinai. The suggestion here seems to be that but for divine help mediated through Moses' uplifted hands, the Amalekites would have prevailed. The Amalekites were fierce enemies of Israel in later times (1 Sam 15) and, against them, the idea of the 'holy war' seems to have arisen—a total war, involving total destruction of the defeated enemy and all his possessions, in the name of Yahweh. Von Rad thinks the holy war was waged only when Israel's very existence was at stake. John Bright thinks the notion covered all Israel's wars, though the conditions were not usually fully applied in practice.

18. Moses and social organisation

When Moses had gone back to Egypt after the encounter at the burning bush he is said to have taken his wife and son (Ex 4). Now his wife and two sons appear with her father Jethro, when he comes to meet Moses. It may have been to smooth this discrepancy that an editor has added at 18:2 that Moses sent his wife away from Egypt. She may have returned to Jethro for safety. Num 12:1 mentions Moses marrying a Cushite—an Ethiopian. This may indicate that Moses like most ot leaders was polygamous; or it could just be another way of describing Jethro's daughter Zipporah. But it is not part of the purpose of the authors to satisfy our curiosity about Moses' personal biography at this level.

The mountain of God is presumably Mt Sinai, otherwise known as Mt Horeb (Ex 3) where Moses learnt Yahweh's name. That the Midianite Jethro now presided
over the sacred meal and advised Moses on the administration of justice in Israel, together with the tradition
that Yahweh called Moses at the Midianite holy place,
has led some to think that the Midianites were worshippers of Yahweh before Israel (see further in section 7,
on Ex 34).

It was natural for Israel to pass, as this chapter does,
straight from worship to the administration of justice.
For Israel, religion and law were one. But the delegation
of authority was necessary as Israel grew. The 'thousands',
etc, of 18:25 suggest the period of the Judges (1200–
1000 BC).

*1. What evidence is there that Yahweh had his worship-
pers before ever Moses and Israel encountered him?*

*2. Yahweh is a jealous God (20 : 5) and claims Israel's
faith exclusively. Does Exodus present Israel as a jealous
people, claiming Yahweh exclusively as their own?*

*3. Does Exodus build up Moses as a great epic hero, or
is he presented realistically and naturally, with human
weaknesses? Does this suggest anything regarding the historical reliability of Exodus?*

*4. Can we explain the origin of the sabbath rest, and
our seven-day week?*

*5. What form did faith, and faithlessness, take in early
Israel? Was that faith similar to Abraham's (Gen 12), and
to Christ's? Is our own like it? In particular, is the faith
of the church today as future-orientated and hopeful as
Israel's was?*

5
The covenant at Sinai
Ex 19:1–24:11

Ex 19:1–20:21. Covenants

The relationship of groups bound together in some way was not uncommonly described in the ancient near east as a covenant. Great states and small tribes alike made treaties. Sometimes a contract on equal terms was accompanied by certain mutual obligations. At other times, major powers like the Hittite king made unequal agreements with minor powers, in which the major power granted friendship and protection in return for obedience, tribute and support. The typical pattern of these unequal 'suzerainty' treaties has been described by G. E. Mendenhall:

(1) The giver identifies himself: 'Thus says the great king . . .' (2) His power and glorious victories are recounted. (3) The obligations the vassal must observe are listed. (4) A copy of the treaty is to be deposited in the national sanctuary, and read out periodically. (5) Deities are invoked as witnesses, and (6) blessings are pronounced for keeping the covenant, and curses for breaking it.

If you look at certain OT passages, you will see the basis for supposing that Israel's covenant with Yahweh finds expression on the model of these treaties: (1) Ex 20:1–2;

(2) Ex 19:4; (3) Ex 20:3–17; (4) Deut 31:9–13; (5) no parallel here, of course; (6) Ex 23:20–33, Deut 27, Josh 8:34.

A key passage for Israel's self-understanding is 19:3–6. Note that God's holiness is dangerous (19:12); that purification involves abstention from sexual relations (19:15); and that the power of Yahweh is evoked by the images of volcano and storm.

Ex 20:2–17. The commandments

The sixteen verses 20:2–17 do not enumerate ten commandments quite clearly. Catholics and lutherans, in their catechisms, have made ten from verses 3–6, 7, 8–11, 12, 13, 14, 15, 16, 17a, and 17b. Anglicans and calvinists arrive at ten from verses 2–3, 4–6, 7, 8–11, 12, 13, 14, 15, 16, and 17. Orthodox judaism today has yet another system, counting verse 2 by itself as the first commandment; and this again differs from the enumeration current in Christ's day. Recently it has even been argued that there were originally twelve commandments.

In Exodus, they are not called commandments only. They are also 'words'—of God. At Deut 5:6 there is another, slightly different version of the ten words, or decalogue, from the later re-writing of Israel's traditions.

Although the words are spoken to a singular 'thou', it is the community of Israel which is addressed. There is no question yet of individuals generally, as distinct from the social group, being told the will of God. In any case, the early OT books lack the clear dichotomies of modern Europe—individual and social, inward and outward, subjective and objective. OT Hebrew has no word corresponding to our inward 'thinking': the nearest equivalents include the connotation of outward action.

Christians have got used to understanding the decalogue in the context of their own social order, and even
as moral instruction given characteristically to children.
Here, the question is, what did it mean to Israel?

Ex 20:2–3

Was Israel monotheistic? The words 'you shall have no
other gods' indicate a polytheistic background. Here and
there in the ot other gods are referred to quite tolerant-
ly, as in Jgs 11:24 which speaks in one breath of Israel's
Yahweh and Moab's Chemosh. The process is visible in
Exodus by which other deities are subordinated to or
identified with Yahweh (4:24–6, 12:23), and in time the
conviction develops that foreign gods are powerless, and
then non-existent (Is 45:5). But in her own *practice*,
Israel was monotheistic from an early period.

Ex 20:4–6

Does this merely amplify 20:2–3? Or, since 20:3 already
excludes foreign deities, perhaps the images now prohib-
ited are images of Yahweh? If this is so, the purpose of
the prohibition is likely to be to rule out a temptation
the ancient world was prone to—to try to wield power
over the deity through images of him.

Ex 20:7

As in an image, so in his name, a deity was somehow
present. So Israel was not to trifle with Yahweh's name.

Ex 20:8–11

The sabbath is to be observed not for any explicit worship, but for rest. Note that Deuteronomy (5:15) gives a

rather different, humanitarian, explanation of this institution.

Ex 20:12

Adults (the command was not addressed to those in child-hood) were to look after ageing parents, who in early nomadic tribes were often left to die by exposure. The second half of the verse makes a practical appeal to self-interest in the matter.

Ex 20:13

'You shall not murder' is the meaning, since the Hebrew word translated 'kill' denotes arbitrary, unlawful killing, whether murder or manslaughter, but not killing in war or by execution.

Ex 20:14

Forbidden was any violation of the public law of marri-age. A man's sexual relations were restricted to his wife, and any female slaves in his household; these were legally potential concubines. The wife was restricted to her husband. Monogamy seems to have been quite general in early Israel, except for kings; one free legal wife, with full rights, to each husband. The commandment was to pre-vent injury in this sphere. (Deut 22:23–24 extends the law to the betrothed: read Mt 1:19 in the light of this.)

Ex 20:15

Since this commandment occurs among others dealing with relationships between persons, and since 20:17 deals with objects, many think this commandment meant

'You shall not enslave, abduct, kidnap, any man'—particularly any free fellow-Israelite.

Ex 20:16

No false evidence was to pervert justice in courts or gatherings to hear cases. 'Neighbour' here means at least any fellow-Israelite with whom one had contact. The question, 'were non-Israelites neighbours?' was never closed in Israel (cf Lk 10:29).

Ex 20:17

'Covet' does not denote merely interior desire. The decalogue hardly takes account of anything so private. 'Covet' includes all plans and moves towards appropriating another's wife or goods, and it is this commandment, after those relating to God and men, which finally comes down to inanimate objects, property.

A further note about the veto on images

This prohibition set Israel drastically apart from all other worshippers of her time. The prohibition unexpectedly reveals Israel's attitude not only towards Yahweh (to whom she was related by his *word*) but also towards the created world. Israel perceived that the use of images, bound up as it was with nature-religions, tended illegitimately to identify this world with God, or at least to blur the boundary between them. Absolute as was Yahweh's power over this world, he was distinct from it, as creator. Israel's abhorrence of images is another way of expressing the doctrine of creation and the transcendence of God, which in turn is another way of expressing the liberation of the created world from any divine or semi-divine occupation. The world is not the abode of deity, as it was for Canaanite Baal worshippers. So, indirectly, man is promoted, as himself the image and likeness of God (Gen 1:26) to dominion over nature. Provided he hears and obeys the word of Yahweh, the world is before him as the scene of his activity.

Harvey Cox (in *The Secular City*, p 30 f) argues that Israel's refusal to make an object of worship, or an absolute, of anything less than Yahweh himself has implications for codes of morality. We now live with the realisation that some of our ethical rules will seem as irrational and outmoded to our descendants as some of our ancestors' practices seem to us. This is a hard thing for some to bear. But it is used to provide a justification for the contemporary world's pluralism or pluriformity of values, according to which moral systems can claim relative, not absolute, validity. The question arises, is this pluralism just a new form of the ancient polytheism against which Israel stood out? Is it a revival of the old tolerant syncretism, threatening the heart of judaeo-christianity, its absolute uniqueness, its revolutionary power to change the world?

Ex 20:22–23:19. The 'covenant code'

The body of case-law which makes up this section belongs to a later date—it reflects not a nomadic but an agricultural society. It is inserted here in the conviction that all law is from Yahweh, and that even detailed regulations follow from the covenant. The rules here govern matters like the freeing of slaves; the death penalty; compensation for injury (including the rule of 'eye for eye', 21:24, making the punishment fit the crime, and placing a limit on vengeance); treatment of dangerous animals;

and lending and borrowing (22 : 25)—there was to be no
usury or interest, because this involves hardship for the
poor, who borrow). One notable feature of this legislation is the humanitarian spirit, most clear at 22 : 21–27.

Ex 23:20–33

This is a separate passage in the style of Deuteronomy,
probably written in a good deal later. It links the fore-
going legislation with the settlement of Canaan. An in-
genious explanation is supplied for the gradual nature of
Israel's infiltration into the promised land (23 : 29). The
writer clearly envisages the maximum extent of Israel's
empire under David as it was in the tenth century.

Ex 24:1–11

This section provides a clear example of the joining of two
stories. Read 24 : 1–2 and 9–11, and then the intervening
verses 3–8. The first source (probably J) tells us the covenant ceremony was carried out by the leaders of Israel in
a sacred meal at the top of the mountain. The second
(probably E) says it was carried out by the people as a
whole, by means of a sacrifice, at the bottom. We naturally ask, which happened? Possibly, both. But perhaps J
is nearer what happened, and E's account is conditioned
by later experience of covenant renewal ceremonies which
took place periodically in Israel. They are enjoined in
Deut 31 : 9–13, and one is described in Josh 24. The
covenant renewal ceremonies usually consisted of an introductory praise of God, a reading of the law, acclama-
tion by the people, and the renewed ratification of the
covenant. Naturally, the Sinai story shaped later covenant
renewal ceremonies. What is less obvious, but no less

true, is that the story of the Sinai covenant ceremony itself, as it now stands in writing, was itself shaped by later renewal festivals.

The two sources in Ex 24 perhaps reflect some dualities —between meal and sacrifice, élite and people, passive reception and active response—which are with us in the church today unresolved.

At this point of covenant-making, it is worth examining the terms Exodus uses to describe Israel, since these are clues to Israel's self-understanding. At 16:1 Israel is a congregation (Heb *edha*, Gk *synagoge*, a gathering together). At 16:3 Israel is an assembly (Heb *qahal*, Gk *synagoge*). Qahal, which often occurs as 'qahal of Yahweh' is sometimes (as in Deut 23:3) translated by the Greek *ekklesia*—those called out and summoned together —which becomes our 'church'. Another term often used for Israel is 'people' (Heb *am*, Gk *laos*)—which often occurs as *laos theou*, people of God. Ex 19:5–6 is more specific. Its description of Israel is appropriated by 1 Pet 2:9 for the christian church.

There is an ambiguity about describing the people of God as a 'kingdom of priests'. Some take it to imply the church's holy apartness from the profane world, its separate development. Others take it to mean that God's people have the role of mediating God's love to the world, being chosen out from the world only in order to be the more dedicated and the more immersed in the world in the service of man—'for all the earth is mine' (Ex 19:5).

1. Is it possible, and permissible, to see in the secular world of the time a basis for Israel's understanding of the covenant relationship with Yahweh?

2. We read in Ex 15:3 that 'Yahweh is a man of war'.

*If such a literary image is permitted, why not pictorial
or carved images?*

3. *Images in worship have occasioned violent strife (in
the maccabean revolt; in the matter of Roman military
standards in Jerusalem; in the eighth century iconoclastic
controversy; in the puritan onslaught on statues). What
is to be said of the crucifix, and other representations of
Christ, and of the use of icons by the orthodox? Where
is the boundary beyond which images become unac-
ceptable?*

4. *Is Israel's imageless worship a foundation of modern
technology through its promotion of human domination
over matter?*

5. *The decalogue seems to have been received in Israel
with joy, as words of life and freedom (cf Deut 30 : 15–
20), not as restrictions. What in Israel's experience helped
her to see the decalogue in this light?*

6. *Books on biblical theology deal with themes like the
election of Israel, the covenant, grace, law, sin, redemption, promise. What are the starting-points, in Israel's
experience, for these doctrines?*

7. *From the names used for Israel, and from her origin
and self-understanding, can any light be thrown on the
true nature of the christian church?*

6
The place of worship
Ex 24:12–31:18 and Ex 35–40

Ex 24:12–31:18

Now, we are told, Moses is summoned up the mountain
to receive the two stone tablets with the commandments
written on them by God (24 : 12, 31 : 18). The story presents him spending forty days and nights on the mountain, being told in detail how to build Israel's place of
worship. The material of this section is practically all
from the Priestly source. P does not see the Sinai event,
as J and E do, primarily as the promulgation of the covenant and the imparting of Yahweh's life-giving law for
the whole of human life. For P, God had already entered
into covenant relation with his people in the time of
Abraham, and even earlier through Noah, and the important thing that happened at Sinai was the inaugura-
tion of legitimate ceremonial worship, the cultic system
by which Israel entered into communion with Yahweh
at the place where he dwelt.

Reading these chapters, we are in a different world.
However old much of the material may be, the authors
(or rather editors and compilers) belong to the sixth
century BC; in some cases even to the fifth. Physically,
they are living in exile in Babylon, but mentally they
stand in Jerusalem where the temple of Solomon had
been till destroyed in 587. The P editors look back to the

thirteenth century, to Moses, and write of Israel's holy place of worship as if it were all one from the thirteenth century to the sixth, or fifth. They see superimposed one upon another, and virtually fused together, the 'tent of meeting' and the 'ark of the covenant'—separate items in the wilderness days; the 'tabernacle' of the early days in Canaan till David; the temple of wood and stone built by Solomon in Jerusalem about 950, and destroyed in 587; perhaps the plans for a new temple envisioned by Ezekiel (in his chapter 40 onwards) which was never built; and perhaps also the second temple built by Zerubbabel in the fifth century after the exile. For P, the differences were not important; the important point was that whether the sanctuary was a tent, a tabernacle, or a temple, Yahweh dwelt with Israel. 'Let them make me a sanctuary, that I may dwell in their midst' (25:8). Present at Sinai in fire and cloud, Yahweh remained present in the place of worship 'enthroned on the praises of Israel' (Ps 22:3).

Details of Solomon's temple can be found at 1 Kgs 6–8. This rectangular building of three components, porch, holy place, and holy of holies, is the model in terms of which P describes how the desert sanctuary is to be built —but for transport in the desert P makes everything collapsible and portable.

Two ideas of the ark compete in the pages of the OT. One is of a portable throne on which Yahweh was invisibly present. The other is of a chest in which the two stone tablets of the commandments were kept. As far as we know, the ark and tablets were in the temple till 587, when they were either destroyed, or hidden for safety and never retrieved. The 'mercy-seat' (25:17) seems to have been the lid of the chest—or the seat of the throne.

When the ark was placed by Solomon in the holy of holies, it was placed between two cherubim, sphinx-like creatures corresponding to angels or protecting powers. The table was for offerings other than sacrificed animals. The seven-branched lampstand seems to have belonged to the second temple (Zech 4:2); Solomon's temple had ten, apparently single, lampstands (1 Kgs 7:49). The lay-out is indicated at 26:33–35. Ex 27 describes the altar of sacrifice, and the surrounding court; 28, the elaborate costume of the high priest; 29, the consecration of priests, and animal sacrifices; 30, the altar of incense—a feature of the second temple; and 31, the godly craftsmen who are to carry out the work. Note (31:14–15) that P regards the sabbath rest as so serious that sabbath-breakers are to be put to death.

Ex 35–40

The instructions given in 25–31 are reported by the concluding chapters (35–40) as executed. Much of 35–40 is identical in wording with 25–31, apart from a change from the future to the past tense. The conclusion to 40, however, is new, and provides such conclusion as Exodus possesses: Yahweh's glory comes down upon the combined tent of meeting and tabernacle, and dwells there continually with Israel (40:34.)

But Exodus does not, really, conclude. The narrative continues with Israel at Sinai all through the next book, Leviticus, and into the following book, Numbers, as far as 10:11. Only then do the pilgrim people of God set out again on their slow nomadic way to the promised land.

1. In parts, Exodus seems to attach great importance to certain places as holy. Is this in accordance with what

Exodus as a whole tells us of God and his way of acting? (Stephen's view in Acts 7 is relevant to this discussion).

2. What is distinctive about P's interpretation of the Sinai event?

3. Martin Noth remarks that the decalogue (Ex 20) reflects a belief that the special relationship of Israel to Yahweh is expressed in obedience to the one God and his demands, not in liturgical worship but in the sphere of social relationships. Do you agree?

7

The temptation of Israel
Ex 32–34

Ex 32

Being different from other peoples was a strain on Israel.
(They felt it again when they demanded to have a king,
like other nations, 1 Sam 8.) In Moses' long absence on
the mountain, they demanded something more tangible
to follow, like the gods of ordinary nations. According to
some, this incident really happened in the wilderness as
narrated; others think it is a tale composed in the tenth
century when the united kingdom split, when King Jeroboam 1 seceded with the northern tribes and set up
shrines in rivalry to Jerusalem. According to 1 Kgs 12 :
28–30, he made two golden calves, which if they did not
stand for Yahweh himself, stood like the ark and the
cherubim at Jerusalem for the presence of Yahweh. Those
who think the story late point to 32 : 4, 'these are your
gods', more appropriate to Jeroboam's two calves than to
Aaron's one, and possibly a quotation from 1 Kgs 12 : 28.

In either case, the story of the golden calf conveys Yahweh's abhorrence of idolatry, to deter Israel from adulter-
ating her worship with the observances of her Canaanite
neighbours. That the story went deep into Israel's consciousness is suggested by the references to it that crop up
in the early church (in Acts 7, and 1 Cor 10).

The strange account of the massacre of the levites

(32 : 25–29) is perhaps to illustrate that tribe's special orthodoxy, and to legitimise its later claim to officiate as priests—it seems that in early times, the head of every family and clan acted as a leader of worship, or priest. The account conveys too the weight of God's demands on Israel's obedience, and the severity of his judgment on apostasy. Meanwhile, Moses' intercession saves Israel from the worst of Yahweh's wrath.

Ex 33

Israel's sin over the calf, and the prospect of departure from Sinai, give grounds for concern about whether Yahweh will remain with his people. Repentance, signified by the putting off of ornaments, mollifies Yahweh, who does not withdraw himself altogether but remains with Israel through his 'presence' (33 : 14–15). Perhaps the suggestion is that in future Israel will encounter and know Yahweh in a mediated way in public worship; only Moses was privileged to have Yahweh speak with him 'face to face, as a man speaks to his friend' (33 : 11).

It seems that Israel early asked the question, what distinguishes her from other nations that Yahweh should choose her as his own? Was it some moral superiority, or some greater responsiveness? Especially after the apostasy of the worship of the calf, the solution could only be found in the free and gratuitous character of Yahweh's gracious choice (33 : 16, 19).

Ex 34

Here is a problem. The story tells of Moses spending yet another forty days on the mountain and receiving the ten words of Yahweh all over again on new tablets. And the

ten words are different words (34 : 10–26). To some extent, the editors have concealed the problem by presenting the new decalogue as part of a new covenant made
necessary by Israel's apostasy over the calf. The decalogue
in 34 concerns matters of worship only, whereas the decalogue in 20 gives commands on ethical matters mainly.
Hence scholars speak of the ritual decalogue (RD) and the
ethical decalogue (ED). The RD strikingly reflects Israel's
life after the occupation of Canaan when they lived side
by side with Canaanites (34 : 11–16) and had settled down
to agriculture (34 : 21–24).

A solution suggested by H. H. Rowley and others is as
follows. The RD is the law of certain of the twelve tribes
who were never in Egypt but migrated directly from
Sinai into Canaan, and who perhaps learnt of Yahweh
through the Midianites or Kenites, and not through
Moses. The ED is the law of the tribes Moses led out of
Egypt. Probably the RD is from J, the ED from E. Another
complication is that the RD overlaps to some extent with
the covenant code in 23. The problem remains unsolved.

When Moses came down, he is said to have covered his
face with a veil. Not impossibly, he followed the custom
of Egyptian priests (and, later, classical actors) in wearing
a mask appropriate to his role.

*1. Did Israel mean the golden calf to represent Yah-
weh, or some other god or gods? Or Yahweh in the form
of another god? (Or did they just not know?)*

*2. There were from the outset failings in Israel, duly
recorded (Ex 17; 32). Does this suggest that even in the
most creative periods, God's people always have failings?
Has the church today failings? If so, ought they to be
talked about openly?*

3. Someone has remarked that modern christians have one thing to be thankful for: however hard they find keeping most of the commandments, they are at least not tempted to worship idols. What do you think?

4. The narrative records Israel's weaknesses candidly. Can anything be inferred from this about the historicity of Exodus, and about the author's purpose?

5. Is it possible to explain why we have one version of Yahweh's commandents in Ex 20, and another in 34?

6. At the exodus period, what made a person a member of the community of Israel? (How today would you define a Jew?)

7. Can we say that Exodus throws light on what God is by showing clearly what he is not?

8

Exodus, the new testament, and the theologising process

The exodus story of God's redemption of his people from slavery, death, and non-being was used as a model by the first christians to explain God's new saving act in Christ. The new covenant, celebrated in the eucharist, is built on the old, celebrated in the passover; and the exodus experience of liberation or redemption is still operative as a basis of the NT experience of salvation. 'Salvation', Jesus told the Samaritan woman, 'is from the Jews' (Jn 4:22).

In the life of Jesus, who in himself represented Israel, the story of the forty days' temptation in the wilderness of Judaea is told upon the pattern of Israel's forty years' temptation in the wilderness of Sinai. Jesus' replies to Satan are taken from the exodus story as re-told in Deuteronomy (8:3; 6:13; 6:16) and the Psalms (106:14; 106:19, 95: 8–9). The temptation to turn stones into bread is related to Israel's murmuring against God when hungry (Ex 16:2–3); the temptation to worship Satan is related to Israel's worship of the calf (Ex 32); and the temptation to manipulate God into working a miracle is related to Israel's faithless testing of God at Massah and Meribah (Ex 17:1–7.)

To examine further the use the NT makes of Exodus, here are some of the chief references: Mt 2:15; 5:21 f; Mk 7:10; Lk 9:31 (where 'departure' is in Greek *ex-*

odos); Jn 5:46, 6:31, 8:58, 19:23–24, 19:36; Acts 7, 13:16 f; 1 Cor 10:1 f, 11:25, 2 Cor 3:7 f; 1 Pet 2:9–10. In addition, the whole of the letter to the Hebrews is relevant—which explains the Christ event in terms of OT worship; and the letter to the Galatians—which deals with the relation of new and old covenants in terms of gospel and law, faith and works, freedom and slavery.

Exodus provides a starting-point from which to examine the theologising process in general. The following outline is put forward for discussion.

1. An event occurs: the exodus escape reveals the action of God, and evokes the response of faith.

2. The event is commemorated, celebrated, proclaimed and interpreted, in regular liturgical acts of worship, at which the implications of the event for life and conduct (commandments and law) are explained, and believers express or renew their commitment.

3. In the liturgical celebrations, God's people encounter him. They are related to him, and so are brought into being actively as a people. And their identity is nourished as the record of the original events is recited and the meaning expounded—as tradition, oral at first, is handed on.

4. The records of the original events, and subsequent developments, are later put into writing, and eventually (when agreed material is separated out from apocryphal) scripture emerges.

5. Liturgical worship is a public proclamation, and a missionary event; and the events are narrated and explained, not only to the faithful community and their children, but also to those not yet in the community who wish to join it.

6. Since man is a reasoning being, he studies and clarifies the revelation he has received, and gives a consistent

and intelligible account of it as far as he can. He himself wants to understand, and he has to teach his children and defend his own belief in the presence of others with different beliefs. So (from the start) theology arises, some of it developing at certain periods into generally accepted doctrine, some even into officially defined dogma.

In recent centuries, since the council of Trent and the protestant reformation particularly, the various aspects of the one christian phenomenon, scripture, tradition, liturgy, revelation, doctrine, mission, religious education, moral teaching, and public witness, have been treated and studied as separate elements, so that the church's life has been rather fragmented and departmentalised. For catholics, 'going to mass' was separated from 'learning the faith' at school. Liturgy became specialised as an activity for monks. Bible reading, if not actually discouraged, became a private affair—though the bible is essentially a public, liturgical book of the church. Established churches organised missions abroad as a separate activity. Revelation came to be thought of as something belonging entirely to the past—a deposit, closed with the death of the last apostle—though in fact much light is thrown on the scene by the immediate current situation in which the church finds itself in the world. For some centuries, many catholics divided up scripture and tradition as distinct sources of revelation—though scripture is tradition, in written form. Protestants tended to elevate scripture above the church—though scripture is the church's possession and creation. Many thought that theologising and the work of formulating doctrine began where scripture ended—though scripture is part (a privileged part) of the interpreting and theologising process. Even the church itself was widely identified, for practical purposes, with the magisterium and administrative organs. That much of this was detrimental to the life of the church was recognised at the second Vatican council.

What is suggested here is that a reading of Exodus in the context of the OT as a whole, and some reflection on the NT, should show the way to overcome this fragmentation and to restore the separated elements to the unity they really constitute as aspects of the one complex reality, the judaeo-christian phenomenon, the life of the people of God.

1. Does Exodus show any similarity in structure and style with any book or books of the NT?

2. Since Vatican II especially, the church has often been described as the 'pilgrim' church (see the document on the church, 8, and 48; and On Ecumenism, 6). What relevance to itself does the church see in the exodus? (There are other references : On Revelation, 14–16; and On Non-Christians, 4.)

3. The gospels are much concerned with conflict over the Jewish law between Jesus and the authorities, and the epistles are much concerned with the relation of the gospel to the law. What is the NT's attitude to Israel's law?

4. Is scripture a consistent, monolithic, body of teaching? Or is there pluriformity of expression, and development of doctrinal and moral teaching, within scripture? What difficulties arise from your answer?

5. The view of many theologians is that God revealed himself through his acts in history—not through the seasonal cycle of nature, nor the mystical experience of the individual soul, nor through any privileged medium like the delphic oracle. Does Exodus confirm this view? Can there ever be enough reliability in the scriptural narratives to make faith secure on this basis?

Deuteronomy

Joseph Blenkinsopp

Introduction
Deuteronomy: the book of the covenant

The title of the book isn't really important, so a subtitle has been added. Even it is no longer all that clear. A covenant is generally understood as a bargain, a compact, or contract. This could take us disastrously wide of the mark at once. There is, however, no acceptable alternative apart from following the Jewish practice of putting down the first word or two of the book as a title, and 'These are the words' if not misleading is not particularly enlightening. One would simply have to begin reading and find out for oneself that a covenant, in the scriptural usage, is a means by which two persons enter into a relationship which is not just casual and on the surface. The friendship of David and Jonathan, for example, which provoked the heart-broken lament in 2 Sam 1, is described as a covenant. It means friendship of a special kind, mutual commitment. Recent studies have suggested that the way the covenant between God and the people of Israel is described in this book has been influenced by the form of political covenants between nations. They have also greatly strengthened the case for the high antiquity of this way of speaking. Here again, this doesn't imply that Israel came to an 'arrangement' with her God. One should remember how the prophets, and especially

Hosea, dynamically re-interpreted the standard terminology, re-stating it in terms of human experience.

Deuteronomy is the fifth and last division of the Jewish *torah* or pentateuch. It is really a law-book, but the law is presented within a framework which gives it a unique sense. This framework is the liturgy of covenant-renewal, the greatest liturgical occasion in the Jewish year. The liturgical character of the book is disguised in historical dress; the preacher hides behind Moses and the congregation behind the Israelite community at mount Sinai or in Moab. It was not of course written by Moses, but contains the essentials of mosaic religion and was in fact put together as the blueprint for a religious reform which aimed at returning upstream to the mosaic origins. There is also evidence that it was composed, at one stage of its literary history, as an ecumenical document, to promote the reunion of divided Israel. This alone must give it some claim on our attention.

We will try in the commentary to pick out what is relevant in this book to our christian life today, and it should encourage us to realise that no other book of the old testament, with the possible exception of Isaiah, has so deeply influenced the new testament (ie the new covenant) as Deuteronomy. We can summarise some of the main points here before we begin:

1. The mystery of God's choice of Israel, a country the size of a couple of English counties, to work out his purposes in the world.
2. The church as a people, the people of God ('the Israel of God'—Paul) which realises its identity by coming together in a liturgical gathering.
3. A community which lives by the word of God and

rejects the magical supernaturalism and *do ut des* type of religion then current in Canaan.

4. A community which accepts the implications of the self-disclosure of God as righteous and social responsibility as the basis of life together.

5. Witness to the prophetic irruption into a closed order and into a religion which aims at making you feel good inside.

6. The liturgical celebration of God's act. This prepares for our understanding of the ministry of Jesus, and especially of his death, the real meaning of which is revealed in the resurrection-faith, as act of God.

Book list

1. *Jerusalem Bible.* Introduction and notes by H. Cazelles.

2. *Peake's Commentary* (2nd ed 1962). A devout commentary by the Baptist scholar G. Henton Davies.

3. There are several other commentaries in circulation, eg, *Torch, Westminster, Clarendon,* most of which have something to offer. They should, however, be used only in an emergency.

4. On the covenant-idea and covenant-theology: W. Eichrodt, *Theology of the Old Testament,* Vol I (in *The Old Testament Library* series) and G. von Rad, *Studies in Deuteronomy* (S.C.M., 1953); on a more popular level B. W. Anderson, *The Living World of the Old Testament* (Longmans, 1958).

5. As a follow-up to the study of Deuteronomy a reading of the *Constitution on the Church,* especially sections 1, 2 and 7, is recommended.

1

Israel on the move
Deut 1:1–3:29

Deut 1:1–18

The book begins with vast panoramic horizons and names like a roll of drums. The scenario is the *araba,* the wasteland between Sinai-Horeb and Transjordania overlooking the land of promise, the country through which the people struggled for forty years and where many of them left their bones. The history here, of course, is idealised —as are the boundaries of the land (1:5), and indeed the whole idea of one people on the march and entering Canaan as a single body. It wasn't really like that at all. The people addressed in the first discourse which begins after the rather complicated introduction (probably three introductions to three different editions rolled into one) is the liturgical assembly of the 'church' of Israel of a much later day than that of Moses. We are not so much concerned here with to what extent, if at all, the ideal for the covenant people was ever realised in history; what is more relevant is to find out what that ideal was and how it can still be relevant for the christian people of today.

After the order to occupy the land we have the important question of the appointment of leaders, scribes, and judges. The people are invited to choose their own leaders who are then invested with office by Moses. A fuller account of this appointment is in Num 11:16–30 from the Northern tradition of which Deuteronomy is the heir and which must be read in connection with Deut 1:9–17. From this we see the prophetic, charismatic source of all authority in the community. In the same way Ex 18:13–27, also Elohist or Northern, must be read in connection with the appointment of judges. This is an excellent model for the practice of subsidiarity in the church which could lead some of our church-leaders to examine their whole attitude to the exercise of authority, if they ever read it!

Organisation is necessary (1000s, 100s, 50s, and 10s), unity is necessary (ultimate appeal to Moses), but neither organisation nor unity is an end in itself—which we too easily forget.

1. How is the unity of the church best expressed liturgically?

2. What are the reasons for thinking that bishops and other church leaders should be chosen 'from beneath' and invested with office 'from above'?

Deut 1:19–33

The Israelites had got through 'the great and terrible wilderness' to the half-way house of the oasis of Kadesh. Some of them must have thought of settling there and it looks as if many traditions preserved in the Pentateuch were formed there, especially those behind the stories in Num 11–20. The order to enter the land, fulfil their destiny, take hold of the promise, is repeated, but they fight shy. The rather odd fact that they balk despite an encouraging report from the scouts sent out in advance is due to an unsatisfactory compression of the fuller story found in Num 13 which could be read at this point.

Anyhow, a crisis of confidence sets in—fortified cities, tall population (remember Semites are on the small side!), and then the ultimate horror, the last straw—'moreover, we have seen *the Anakim* there!'— better stay put. God had promised them the land, 'yet, in spite of this word, you did not *believe* . . .' Faith means confidence, the courage to give oneself, 'the courage to be' (Tillich). Faith in God for the Deuteronomists means taking God at his word, looking for security and strength *only there*! Some spurious substitutes for this faith will come up for comment later. When this faith is absent, God's promise is turned upside down, his motives are questioned: 'Because the Lord hated us he has brought us out of the land of Egypt'—for Deuteronomy the basic conviction is that 'it is because the Lord loves you that he has brought you out with a mighty hand' (7 : 8). The church could not exist without this faith.

In a verse which was probably added on to the address at some later stage, we read of God carrying his people 'as a man bears his son' (1 : 31). Back in Egypt he says to Moses: 'Israel is my first-born son. Tell Pharaoh: "let my son go that he may serve me" ' (Ex 4 : 22–23). It is almost impossible for us to imagine the newness, the strangeness of this language of human relationships when first used (of Israel) by the prophets and their disciples. It is just one indication of the strong prophetic undercurrent in this book, which in this case probably goes back to the Northern prophet Hosea ('Out of Egypt have I called my son!' 11 : 1, cf Mt 2 : 15). It reminds us of God's providence for his church in what he has done, in leading it out, and in what he will do, in gathering it together.

1. How is God's call to Israel to enter the land typical

of his call addressed to the church today to enter the
world? Has this brought on a new crisis of faith?

2. How are we to understand Christ's sonship and ours
as christians in the light of Hosea and Deuteronomy?

Deut 1:34–46

The preacher's language of a good part of Deuteronomy,
especially evident here—the anger of God, the men of
this evil generation, and the like—points to the liturgical
origins of the book. The history, and a great deal of old-
testament history outside of this book, acquired its present form through continual repetition in the liturgical
recitals of Passover and the other festivals. History is not
recited in the liturgy for its own sake—it is God's act, his
apologia, and Israel's collective examination of conscience
as a prelude to conversion. This explains a psalm like
106, which should be read in connection with this passage, and why the major theme of both is the extreme
cantankerousness of Israel. The technical term for this in
Deuteronomy is *rebellion* (1 : 45) because this was part
of the idiom of covenant-making and covenant-breaking
in which the book was conceived. How is our history as
a church different from this?

We might add that this idea of the 'anger' of God,
being metaphorical or mythological (but none the less
real!), is a rather hard one for us to accept. This is especially true here since the anger of the Lord against Moses
seems capricious and pointless. It may make it easier if
we note that the story of the water-miracle in Num 20,
which is behind 37, was probably not attached (originally) to the punishment of Moses at it is now. The real
trouble seems to have been that the southern tribes, who
eventually entered the land from the south, fell out with

those of the North whose story is told in Joshua, and that
this 'fall out' is here given a theological interpretation.
And since Deuteronomy is the blue-print for a 'back to
Moses' reform, it was natural that he shouldn't be blamed
(the Lord was angry with him 'on your account'! cf 3:
26). Be that as it may, what is of first importance is 'wholly
to follow the Lord'—total commitment, not getting
caught half-way. And that, when we come to think of it,
is the trouble with being a christian: you have to be in
it 100 per cent, you have to go the whole hog, or condemn yourself to increasing frustration and end up in
unreality and insincerity.

*1. What light does the insistence on the recital of
Israel's history throw on the function of church history
today, with special reference to 'ecumenical repentance'?*

*2. What meaning can you give to the expression 'the
anger of God'?*

Deut 2:1–3:11

In this longer section the preacher has summarised the
ancient and sometimes mutually discordant traditions
about the wanderings of the Israelites for forty years
around the oasis of Kadesh and in the burnt-up, god-
forsaken land south of the Dead Sea. A later hand has
added various more or less erudite notes about the ancient, prehistoric populations of those regions such as the
Zamzummim and museum pieces such as Og's bed, very
likely a fallen slab of a pre-historic monument. We need
not linger lovingly over these. What is interesting is the
sense of providence (is this still a viable expression?) in
the apparently random movements and events of history.
Israel is told: you didn't know it, but the Lord was with

you in that dark period, you were *known*, there was a pattern (2 : 7). But God's providence is not just for Israel: he has allotted land to other, often hostile, countries such as Edom, Moab, and Ammon. This idea was rooted in Canaanite mythology, as can be seen in 32 : 8–9 where El the supreme god allots peoples to the other divine beings *including Yahweh!* It was demythologised by the prophets and is made use of here. This idea of God acting outside of the covenant and the covenant-people has not yet been fully absorbed by the christian church. Deuteronomy was too absorbed with national revival to see it clearly, and so we have to look elsewhere in the old testament—the Servant Songs in particular—for the beginnings of an answer. Tillich writes: 'Yahweh revealed Himself through Israel's pain as the God who is the first and the last, the beginning and the end, of history. A complete national breakdown alone made the remnants of Israel ready to receive this revelation in its universal significance. But whenever the Jewish nation used that revelation as an excuse for national pride, and transformed Yahweh into a purely national god, another breakdown followed. For Yahweh as a national god is always condemned by Yahweh the God of history.' (*The Shaking of the Foundations,* Penguin, 1962, pp. 39–40.) Because the main edition of Deuteronomy was written for a projected revival it has about it a certain at times savage triumphalism (as here) which was to be rudely shattered by the unforeseen course of events. In a time when we are talking a lot about revival within the christian communions maybe this points to a danger which we haven't altogether succeeded in avoiding.

1. How should we see the connection today between

the providence of God within the covenant and outside it?

2. *To what extent is nationalism compatible with christian commitment?*

Deut 3:12–29

We have here a very much abbreviated and stylised summary of the account of the settlement of the Transjordan tribes in Num 32. Even though separated from the west-bank tribes they still formed a unity with them, and so had the duty to take part in the conquest until all the tribes had settled down. This conviction of a predestined unity which had to be maintained at all costs and had to be expressed in common action is very impressive. So, for example, the largest tribe, Manasseh, was divided into two in order to maintain the number 12, the sign of unity. This reminds us that the very first christian meeting was called to pick a twelfth man to take the place of Judas who had fallen out (Acts 1 : 15–26). The whole point of the reform of Josiah in the late seventh century BC, which was based on Deuteronomy, was to re-establish unity between the broken-up tribes. Though the ideal was realised only very imperfectly at any time, and only fully (more or less) for a lifetime under the united monarchy of David and Solomon, it was never abandoned. The fact that the preacher in Deuteronomy addresses one united people shows us how this unity must be expressed in the liturgical gathering; and the fact that the liturgical meeting is taken up so much with remembering, *anamnesis*, shows us that this in its turn is based on living together, sharing in one history. Unity cannot be created just by willing it; nor can it be achieved once and for all. It has to be fought for all the time.

Moses' prayer (3 : 23–25) is a first run-through for the 'high utterance' of the levitical preaching we shall be hearing at full spate in the next chapter. By the end of the chapter we have arrived at the end-point for the doomed desert-generation (of which Moses was part) and the starting-point for the new generation of the settlement in the good land. It is here that the law for life in the land is given. It is here that Moses speaks (1 : 5), that he saw the land and then died.

Can liturgy be a means of promoting christian unity or should it be regarded as essentially the expression of a unity already acquired?

2

The meaning of the law
Deut 4:1–43

Deut 4:1–14

The 'and now' shows that the historical prologue is finished and we are getting down to business, for we find the same thing in political 'covenants' or treaties elsewhere in the ancient Near East. What follows is an explanation of the meaning of the law. At first blush, it might look like a morality for mercenaries: that you may have long life in the land; lest it happen to you as to those who sinned at Baalpeor (the incident narrated in Num 25 is referred to). Obey the law or else. This is because the author—and his contemporaries—knew of no moral order separate from the material and physical order. There was but one order at the same time divine and human, spiritual and physical. Law is essential to this order and its observance promotes life at every level. Law is not a burden but a gift; it is for the Hebrew the primary aspect of God's self-communication and self-giving; it is synonymous with wisdom and understanding (4:6). Here we should read how later judaism spoke of the law as a divine reality, in Prov 8:22–34 and Sir (Ecclesiasticus) 24—passages which the Roman liturgy has applied, by accommodation, to the Virgin.

The law is the revelation of a personal God since law presupposes will and will is the highest function of per-

sonality. It expresses therefore God's freedom and invites
observance as the way to personal freedom, not the contrary as one might at first suppose. This self-revelation
means that Yahweh is *the God who is near*, a theme often
repeated in Deuteronomy (and in the Deuteronomic History—for example, the prayer of Solomon, 1 Kgs 8 : 10 ff).
God is not a life force, an impersonal energy. For the
author he does not come near through spiritual ecstasy (as
in Greece) or sexual ecstasy (as in Canaan) but by making
himself present through his word to a believing community. This encounter is a mystery expressed in Deuteronomy by the imagery of fire, the fire of the burning
mountain (read Heb 12 : 18–24, a splendid transposition
to the christian mystery of encounter). Those of us in the
church today who have forgotten this *demonic* element in
the scriptural god, who have opted for a tame god on a
string, should ask ourselves what it means that he is described as being angry and jealous, that he suffers passion
and pain. Can God really be like this?

We should note once again the strong liturgical character of this book. Those addressed are the liturgical
community, 'you, all of you, who are alive this day' (cf
the deuteronomic Ps 95, 'O that *today* you would hearken
to his voice!' and Heb 3 : 7–11). 'The day that you stood
before the Lord your God' (4 : 10) is the day of the liturgical assembly; in fact the Greek version adds: 'on the
day of the assembly (*ekklesia*)'. The role of memory,
anamnesis (4 : 9), points in the same direction. This reminds us of 'all those who stand about' in the prayer of
institution and the cultic remembrance of the death of
the Lord, '*Unde et memores, Domine . . .*' which is the
centre of our eucharistic service.

   1. In what way can new-testament law be regarded as a covenant-law?

   2. Is it still possible for us, more than twenty-five centuries later, to accept Deuteronomy's image of God?

   3. For Deuteronomy 'the church' is a liturgical term— how can we do our rethinking at this end, rather than at that of the church as an abstract concept imperfectly embodied in a collection of people?

Deut 4:15–31

This is a commentary on the first two of the ten commandments, a homily about idolatry, with the objects of idolatry in the same order as in the commandments which follow soon after (5:6 ff). This was the main element in the Josian reform (see 2 Kgs 23:4 ff) with which Deuteronomy is associated, as we saw. The list starts with the human form (the fertility gods and goddesses), and then from beast (the bull), bird (the falcon of Horus), creeping things (the Canaanite snake-god), and fish (Leviathan and the other monsters of the Abyss) to the heavenly bodies worshipped especially in Mesopotamia. The exilic insertion of 4:25–31 attributes all the disasters of Israel to idolatry, and we get the point clearly if we read Ezek 8, the prophet's guided tour through the temple on the eve of the exile, and Gen 1, the Priestly creation recital in which the polemical note against idolatry is easy to detect.

   We tend to think of idolatry as something childish and primitive, chiefly because it is so difficult for us to enter into the mind of people living so long ago. They were not so silly as just to worship a bull; for them the bull was the symbol and vehicle of the whole blind procreative power within the natural order. Their worship had the object of inserting man fully into that order. Basically, idolatry is a search for security, a return to the natural order which man transcends and in which he can never feel entirely at home. For the Hebrews, and especially for the Deuteronomists, it was a refusal of a unique destiny. At its worst it becomes a form of self-worship, confirmed by Jung who tells us that the *ego* has the same numinous quality which traditional theologies ascribe to God. Yahweh, unlike these other gods, is spiritual and personal and demonstrates his personalism in free acts, most of all in the creation of a real community out of what had been just a bunch of slaves (4:20). The other gods were content to have their own spheres of influence; Yahweh was *a jealous God* who could stand no rival, he and he alone was *the living God*.

The tendency to idolatry is constant throughout history though the object or form of our idolatry changes constantly. Therefore there is a constant need to *return* to the Lord (4:30). This is the verb which the Greek translators render by *metanoeō*, implying a radical change in one's way of thinking, a change of direction, repentance.

1. To what extent is idolatry still a live issue today for christians?

2. Can we really worship God without images of the kind we find here— for example as 'the ground of being'?

Deut 4:32–43

This is one of the high-points of the deuteronomic homily. The act of God which constitutes Israel's gospel is the centre of all time ('from the day that God created man upon the earth') and space ('from one end of heaven to the other'). This self-disclosing of God is something mysterious like fire. Its strangeness lies in the fact that, while the history of religions tells us about man's search for God, the old testament is the story of God's search for man, for a people. Its starting-point is not a concept or a religious idea but a social experience ('to you it was shown', 4:35). The love of God can mean different things to different people at different times. We now know that 'love', *hesed,* was at that time a technical cove-nant-making term expressing the benevolence of a ruler in granting a covenant or treaty to an unequal. Here, in Deuteronomy, it receives concrete expression in God's choice of a people, the doctrine of election. This is the starting-point for our christian doctrine of grace, which should not be thought of as a sort of juice which is pumped into people subject to the performance by them of specific acts. Grace in biblical terms is an event, God coming to us in salvation.

A passage like this gives us the lead for understanding what is the centre of the christian gospel. It is God's final act wrought in Christ. The public ministry is defined in the first christian homily as 'the mighty works and won-ders and signs which God did through him' (Acts 2:22), the God of our fathers raised him from the dead (Acts 3:13), God is reconciling the world to himself in Christ (2 Cor 5:19). This is experienced by the apostolic com-munity (hence the need for witness) and the cultic re-creation of this experience in the liturgy makes the christian community what it is.

The moral or legal side of covenant-making has to be seen in this context of revelation, as is clear from the *therefore* of 4:40. We shall, however, have to discuss this more thoroughly at a later stage. The final bit about the setting up of cities of sanctuary(like the mediaeval idea) looks out of place here, cf 19:1–14, and, in any case, is not important for us, so we can pass on with a good conscience.

To what extent have we in the west (unlike the eastern church) given too little place to experience in our christian life? What could be meant, for the christian, by 'religious experience'?

3

The ten words: law or love?
Deut 4:44–6:25

Deut 4:44–5:22

The liturgical promulgation of the covenant-law, the ten words, is introduced in the rest of Chapter 4, by a preface of the expanding type that we saw at the beginning of the whole book. 4:47–49 is a learned gloss added later by some scholar or other which can be skipped. The official promulgation begins with the call to the congregation to listen (5:1, as also 4:1 and 6:1). Here we are in the liturgy of covenant-renewal at a religious centre in Canaan: the levitical preacher is Moses, the congregation is the people of God at Sinai-Horeb. Something of this is true of the christian covenant-renewal, the eucharist, of which Christ is the one mediator (Heb 9:15).

There are two 'editions' of the ten words (as they are called both here and in Exodus); the other comes in the last edition of the Pentateuch (Ex 20:2–17) put together by the priests, but both go back to a much earlier and briefer form. Originally they would all have been of the short sharp type like 'Thou shalt not kill!', but in the course of time were worked over and expanded homiletically. So, for example, sabbath-observance is enjoined in the two editions for different reasons. It was probably quite common to write up laws in decades and there are other examples in the old testament. The law is authenticated by the pious fiction that it is written by God, a good illustration of which can be seen in the Hammurapi column in the Louvre on which we see the god handing the law-code to the king, having presumably written it himself. All this is part of the relatively unimportant framework in which the commandments are presented.

There is a problem here for the christian. Jesus, in enjoining observance of the commandments, six of them at any rate, on the rich young man, stated that they are capable of bringing life, eternal life (Mk 10:17–22 and parallels). This was good Jewish doctrine, but is it still true for the christian? Paul didn't seem to think so. Can we say that the christian gets rid of the trappings, cultic and otherwise, and is left with what is of permanent moral obligation in the commandments? And is this hard core found in the ten commandments—are we at least here on the bedrock of 'natural law'? This seems to be the assumption of those christian bodies which expound them in their moral manuals and catechisms. But in what way are perjury or breaking the sabbath against the 'natural law'?

A closer look at the way the ten words come to us here will perhaps show that we have exaggerated the difference between old and new testament with regard to moral teaching, 'code morality' and 'wisdom morality'. They are preceded by a declaration of identity as with all covenant-laws; the lawgiver is also the saviour, the God of the exodus. The law is therefore not an imposition but a gift, a showing of 'steadfast love' to 'those who love me and keep my commandments' (cf Jn 14:15, 'If you love me you will keep my commandments'). Law-observance, obeying precepts, is therefore always, ideally, in function of something greater, an expression of the commitment which is *the* basic covenant-quality. Too often a christian will say in effect: 'Tell me what to do and what not to do and, for the rest, my life is my own' and he might in fact observe laws without any commitment at all in the centre of his life. True christianity is something entirely different from this.

1. In what way if at all do the ten commandments still retain any binding authority?

2. How does the sermon on the mount avoid substituting a new code of law for that of the old testament which is superseded?

Deut 5:23-33

The backcloth for Moses as mediator between the God in the fire and the people is the theophany described in Ex 19. Exactly how relevant the language of the numinous is in our age of pop art and the drama of social comment is a question which may well be asked. Does religion correspond to certain emotional responses; awe, reverence, dependence, the feeling for the numinous, as Rudolph Otto maintained (in *The Idea of the Holy*)? If so, it might be argued that it is condemned to recede as man's rational control of his environment progresses and be confined to fewer and fewer people who in this respect are specially gifted (or psychologically abnormal?). Whatever else we can charge old testament religion with, it was not at any rate designed as a way of emotional release!

The request of the people for a mediator shows us the beginnings of a theology of ministry in the church of Israel. The mediation of Moses is the paradigm for the office of mediation in the history of the community, exercised by priest and prophet. The prophets continue to mediate the word of God (see 18:15 ff), the priest-levites are the instruments of encounter with the covenant-God in sacrifice and the liturgy (see 18:1 ff). In Moses prophet and priest are combined (he came of the family of Levi) which is true also of Christ described in the new testament as prophet and priest. This will concern us more in detail later.

1. What is the relation between the priestly and the prophetic elements in the church today?
2. Where have all the prophets gone?

Deut 6:1-19

After another expanded introduction (there seems no end to them!) there follows the central statement of Israel's faith and commitment, what was afterwards to be called the *Shema*, 'Hear, O Israel!' (6:4–9). This confession, recited by the great rabbi Akiba as he died at the hands of the Roman torturers, and then millions of times during the incessant pogroms in christian Europe, in Treblinka and the Warsaw ghetto, was described by Christ as the first law of the Kingdom. The confessional element is difficult to translate; we should perhaps English it as 'Yahweh is our God, Yahweh alone'—faith in the one god who is *the living God*, who has been the object of collective experience in the Exodus and in comparison with whom the other gods, the gods of the fertile earth and the sky, are dead (this idea of living = operative, dead = inoperative comes out well in the story of Elijah on mount Carmel in 1 Kgs 18). This is confirmed by the homiletic explanation which follows in 6:10–19. No one in the old testament ever tries to *prove* this by rational argument; the appeal is always to experience, and especially to social experience. We can perceive Israel's uniqueness within the historical process. Martin Noth, in many ways a radical critic of what used to be the accepted reconstruction of the history of Israel, wrote towards the beginning of his *History*: 'At the very centre of the history of "Israel" we encounter phenomena for which there is no parallel at all elsewhere, not because the material for comparison has not yet come to light but because, so far as we know, such things have simply never happened elsewhere.' Yet even *we* authenticate Israel not by historical enquiry but by accepting the invitation to participate as part of the same prophetic history. This is the secret of the prodigious strength which this confession has generated throughout the ages.

The homiletic development presupposes the sad experience of what happened when Israel came from the desert into the fertile land of Canaan with its sex-soaked fertility religion. We might think of a young country girl from the west of Ireland who comes to settle in London, a comparison of which one imagines Hosea at any rate would have approved. In the land the fertility gods and goddesses were near and it was only too easy to forget what had happened *outside* the land. In Hosea and Jeremiah, with whom Deuteronomy has strong affinities, this situation is described in predominantly sexual imagery as, for example, when they speak of 'fornicating after strange gods'. The mythological texts discovered in Syria, the hundreds of terracotta figurines of the nude fertility-goddess, the sexual organs often obscenely accentuated, give colour to this way of speaking. How was Israel to remain faithful?

The only way is total commitment: 'with all your heart, with all your soul, with all your strength'. The essence of the covenant lies not in keeping this or that stipulation but in this total commitment at the centre.

That is why christianity could reject the old testament law as a system, a way of life, and yet still be a covenant. Moreover, the one law which summarises all the rest (Mt 22:37) is not really a law at all—you can't really command someone to love God! This should surely be the starting-point for any understanding of christian morality as presented in the new testament and which is so often misrepresented nowadays.

1. How is the biblical way of establishing the reality of God still a live option? What is wrong with rational argument and 'proofs'?

2. To what extent does the relationship of Israel to the land which it enters tell us something about relationship to 'the world' which we would rather not listen to or at least which we tend to play down?

Deut 6:20–25

This passage deserves separate consideration and reading since, with 26:5–11, it shows us how 'theology' in the old testament has its roots in liturgy—both passages are liturgical recitals in which, to some extent at least, the old canonical way of speaking at the great religious festivals in old Israel has been preserved. This is the passover *haggada*, the answer made to the youngest present who asks the age-old question, as is still the case at the Jewish passover supper. It was around this liturgical nucleus that the passover story in Exodus was built up (see chapters 12–13 in particular). The passover is a memorial service and so is the eucharist ('Do this as my memorial service', Lk 22:19). Both look back to an event in the past. Both also express faith in the future. Why did God create a new people in Egypt? To give them the land. Why did he give them the land? To place them as a sign and an instrument of the divine purpose for the nations of the world. What is God's plan for the world? That of it he may make a new and final community of which our several eucharistic communities are, as we christians believe, the pattern.

How is the passover-aspect of the eucharist really relevant to the place the eucharist has in our christian life today?

4

The lessons of Israel's past
Deut 7:1–11:32

Deut 7:1–26

The holy war, rules for which are laid down here, is one
of the least attractive aspects of the life of the covenant-
people even when we put it in perspective—which is not
always done. It was not of course peculiar to the Hebrews; the Moabite stone, discovered last century in
Transjordania, speaks of a holy war of Moab *against* the
Hebrews and the jihad, or holy war of Islam, is well
known. This, of ocurse, doesn't justify the wholesale
slaughter involved, especially when it is carried out at the
express command of a god who is elsewhere described as
a god of love and mercy. What we have to bear in mind
is that, at the time of writing, the holy war was just a
theory conscripted by the writer or preacher in his struggle for reform against idolatry, and even the rather re-
volting section of the book of Joshua (chapters 10–11 in
particular) which describes it in full swing is highly
stylised and theologised—a much truer picture of what
really happened is available in the first chapter of Judges.
At the same time, in view of the fatal tendency of christians to isolate texts and interpret them as separate
oracles, it has had some unfortunate, not to say disastrous,
effects. Reference to the old testament holy war idea and
'the Lord of hosts' has been used to justify crusades

against Moslems, Jews, Albigensians, and others, and the wholesale and indiscriminate slaughter which usually followed. Examples of this kind of thinking can be found in Stanley Windass' *Christianity versus Violence*. We should recall Paul Tillich's words, quoted above, about Israel's mission to the world which could be fulfilled only when she discovered that her national god was too small and was, from one point of view, just a projection of her own destructive instincts and will-to-power.

From one point of view. What is of permanent significance in the holy war idea in Deuteronomy is that it is used to emphasise Israel's *holiness*. The root meaning of this word is *separation*, being chosen, set aside 'out of all the peoples that are on the face of the earth' (7:6). The redemptive love of God for his people (7:8) is an absolutely prior act which sets this people aside so that they can never be just like the others. Newman is true to this biblical insight when he speaks of the church as a community in the process of separation from the world, and, if this is so, we should perhaps speak not of the church's immersing herself or disappearing in the world (phrases often heard nowadays) but of her *re-entry* into it. This is the point of 1 Pet 2:9–10, the description of the church as 'a chosen race, a royal priesthood, a holy nation, God's own people', which derives from the same old-testament theological tradition as Deuteronomy (Ex 19:5–6).

The fight against idolatry was essential to the very existence of Israel. It wasn't a straight fight between Yahweh and the *ba'alim*, the fertility gods of the land—it was a bit more subtle than that. When Jeroboam set up the bull-cult in the north after the break-up of the kingdom he is reported as saying: 'Behold your gods, O Israel, who brought you out of the land of Egypt' (in 1 Kgs 12:28). It was still Yahweh, the name was the same, but the nature had shifted and sometimes the shift was of a rather subtle kind. The issue was between regarding God as a free agent, a person experienced in a mysterious encounter which was only possible through listening to his word, and as a magical force, a god who produced the goods, who gave quick results. This is the theme of Hosea and, following him, of Deuteronomy, and once the point had been made they both could go on to say that the blessing of fertility, of abundance of life also on the physical level, came as a free gift from Yahweh, not as the result of cultic manipulation. This is the point of the blessings in this chapter and with which we can compare Hosea, Chapter 2.

1. How much are the christian churches doing to combat violence and war-psychology? Anyway, is christianity really a religion for pacifists?

2. What signs are there that we have played down the element of holiness, separation, in the christian vocation in recent years?

Deut 8:1–20

Now we are back in the desert. This was the time when God tested his people. There are two quite different forms of temptation, that of the desert and of the fertile land, the temptation of too little and too much. The testing of Jesus in the desert is presented in the gospel as the testing of the people of God, as can be seen from the three quotations from Deuteronomy, the first from this chapter (8:3). The alternatives are: on the one hand to live by God's word, listening, obedience (in Hebrew there is only one verb for 'listen' and 'obey'); on the other, supernatural gimmickry, treating God as a magical power which can be exploited. We do not need to think very hard to realise how real this temptation has been in our christian history. Paul makes the same point basically in his little 'allegory' on the People of God in the desert (1 Cor 10): they were all 'dipped' in the water, they all ate the wonderful bread and drank the wonderful drink, that is, they were all baptised and 'went to' the sacraments but—the sting in the tail—'with most of them God was not pleased'. This is really what the homily in this chapter of Deuteronomy is about.

The temptation of the good land is that of forgetting God the giver and therefore of falling into an idolatrous worship of the products of civilisation. This idolatry is ultimately self-idolatry: 'My power and the strength of my hand have gotten me this wealth' (8: 17). Canaan was the Israelites' welfare-state (as Henton Davies called it in *Peake*) which might lead us to ask whether the same danger besets us as beset the Israelites: setting one's sights on affluence, on getting into the super-tax bracket, regarding oneself as a saleable object and others as potential financial or professional rivals. All of this saps the courage to give oneself without which community is impossible. This is the lesson that Israel had to learn the hard way.

1. How much is there in practice still an element of magic in the way some of us think of the sacraments and of the magician in the way we think of God?

2. Should we continue to say grace before and after meals? (see 8 : 10!)

Deut 9:1–29
The homily continues much in the same vein. The

general tendency to go into a coma when a preacher gets exhortatory or denunciatory may affect us here, but there are some points which deserve our attention.

The re-telling of the account of Israel's apostasy at Horeb (the first version, which could be looked at here, is in Ex 32) presents it not so much as a historical event but rather as an archetypal situation for Israel. The old covenant had been broken—signified by the breaking of the tablets by Moses which act had, in political 'covenants' of that age, a juridical significance. The fact that Deuteronomy was written for a ceremony of covenant-renewal points to the fact that the old covenant was continually broken and had to be continually renewed. Gradually the idea dawned that it was no longer a viable instrument of God's purpose with his people and, through them, with the world; and so a new covenant is promised (in Jer 31:31ff). The covenant-promise: 'I will be their God and they shall be my people' is fulfilled in the christian church. This explains the gospel-presentation of Christ as a Moses-figure: both fast forty days and nights, both give the law on a mountain, both are transfigured, both lead their people from slavery (Luke calls the death of Christ an exodus, 9:31), and so on. It is nothing short of amazing that this fundamental scriptural category of covenant has had no part at all in our potted-theology courses for all these years!

Deuteronomy amplifies the original Horeb-story in various ways (the telling of this story has been much influenced by the apostasy of the northern kingdom with its bull-cult, as can be seen by comparing Ex 32 and 1 Kgs 12), most strikingly by the prayer of Moses (9:25–29). In speaking to God he is not above a little not too subtle arm-twisting, but his prayer is mainly one of intercession. It presupposes that sin and the anger of God mean

something and are not to be demythologised! Sin is here
considered not anthropologically but as the breaking of
a personal relationship and the dissolution of community
ties leading to isolation, what we might prefer to call alienation, not belonging. Then Moses prays: 'Do not destroy thy people whom thou hast redeemed.' Just as we
have tended to individualise the idea of sin, so also that
of redemption. Scripturally, *the* act of redemption is the
exodus from Egypt and, superimposed upon this, that
from Babylon after the exile. This is the basic pattern
for the new testament presentation of the redemptive
death of Christ. By this we are redeemed *as a people*.

*1. How can we make this covenant category really
meaningful for the theological understanding of our
faith?*

*2. Christians have tended for centuries to 'individu-
alise' excessively the idea of sin and of redemption. How
can we deepen our understanding of both by relating
them more closely to the community idea?*

Deut 10:1–11:1

Moses receives the command to make the ark as a con-
tainer for the covenant-law newly written out, whence it
is called in Deuteronomy and the deuteronomic literature the 'Ark of the Covenant'. The levites are appointed
to minister in the ark-sanctuary. There is still a great
deal obscure in the origins and history of both ark and
levites which fortunately we are not called upon to enter
into here. The writer, who was probably himself a levite,
is giving us to understand that they, the levites, had
nothing to do with the apostasy of Aaron since Aaron

was already dead and buried before they were instituted. Having got the point, we can press on.

In the rest of the passage, from 10:12, we have a fine statement on what living within the covenant was to mean, what were to be the basic attitudes. Note how it begins and ends with the attitude to the covenant-God and in the middle there are the specifically moral implications written in large letters for all to read: justice exercised with absolute impartiality, concern for the deprived classes which at that time were chiefly the fatherless, widows, and aliens or immigrants. Comparison with some prophetic passages suggests that behind passages like this there was a sort of covenant-catechism; for example, in Mic 6:8 we find: 'He has shown you, O man, what is good. What does the Lord require of you but to do justice, love kindness and walk humbly with your God?' A careful reading of the passage will show that we have here already two of the basic elements of christian morality: (i) interiority—the phrase about circumcising the heart (see what Paul says in Rom 2:25–29); (ii) social concern—have you ever noticed that judgement in the great judgement-scene in Mt 25:31–46, with the judge on his throne and the imagery of sheep and goats (which we find also in the contemporary Book of Henoch) has to do *exclusively* with social justice and concern?

1. How does this passage help us to understand the now current distinction between a 'code-morality' and a 'wisdom-morality'?

2. Individual christians are generally aware of the need for social concern; but how should christian bodies show this concern in a world where, for example, one in three suffers from hunger and malnutrition?

Deut 11:2-17

Again the historical recital. The Hebrew here takes on a
rhythmic quality which makes one wonder whether the
writer hasn't incorporated old liturgical material into his
story as Paul often does in his letters. We should try to
find time to look at those magnificent covenant-psalms,
many of which come from deuteronomic circles. A list of
the principal ones is appended at the end of the section to
make this easier. They show us how sacred history, what
we now like to call salvation history, is rooted in liturgical recital.

The homily continues with the theme of the good
land. Canaan did not, like Egypt, depend on irrigation,
and therefore on slave-labour, but on a regular supply of
rainfall which determined the local religion just in the
same way as the Central American Indians base all their
religious practice ultimately on the cultivation of the
maize crop (for them christianity is mostly an emotional
luxury though it has brought one more god to placate).
For the Israelite man-in-the-street the question was:
could a desert- and/or mountain-god survive in this
different setting? Similarly, at the exile the question became: could a national god survive in a world which had
suddenly begun to expand beyond belief? Maybe this
problem isn't quite obsolete yet! When we read this
passage we should remember that the people addressed
here were not all able to say with Job: 'even though he
should kill me, yet will I believe in him'. Their god
showed that he was real, that he was with them, by sending the rains, a point which comes out very well in the
contest of Elijah with the four hundred and fifty prophets
on mount Carmel (1 Kgs 18).

Reading the Covenant Psalms

114   Exodus (for the feast of passover)

106 ⎫
135 ⎭ Exodus to Canaan

78   Exodus to David

105   Abraham to Exodus

136   Creation to Canaan ('for his love endures for ever!')

[These show us how the historical traditions of the Pentateuch were built up on a liturgical basis, cf Deut 26: Jacob to Canaan and Josh 24: Abraham to Canaan (the great covenant-renewal of Shechem).]

1. How does a reading of the covenant recitals in Deuteronomy and of the covenant hymns in the book of Psalms help us to understand the nature of liturgical prayer?

2. How should our liturgical prayer take into account the changed condition of people living in an urbanised and industrialised society?

Deut 11:18–32

The address is evidently being wound up here—with the often repeated command to keep alive the covenant tradition until the next ceremony of renewal and the insistence that the law is a law for life in the land of Canaan. We know from comparative material that political treaties or covenants usually ended with more or less stereotyped blessings and curses, the latter thought of as sanctions in the event of non-fulfilment of the covenant stipulations, and sanctions which everyone took seriously. If we don't like this idea of cursing we ought at least to ask ourselves: what other kind of sanction *could* there

be at that time for the weaker partner in such a treaty?
What they express is commitment. The detailed list
comes later (27:11–28:46) and, reading it, as we that in
entering the covenant Israel really burnt her boats! In
this way being an Israelite (as being a christian) isn't like
being a member of a club; you had to make a once-for-all
decision, take it or leave it. The idea of the two ways
which comes later on (30:15) and which is taken up in
new testament times also expresses the need for decision
and commitment.

Gerizim and Ebal are hills on either side of the city of
Shechem, the city which has been called 'the uncrowned
queen of Palestine' and which was the centre of the
northern tribes in which the covenant idea developed (an
American team is digging it up at the moment). In Josh 24
we find the text of a covenant-liturgy which took place
there before the monarchy.

*Doesn't the fact of infant baptism rather blur the effect
of this covenant-idea applied to our christian faith?*

5

Religious and community laws
Deut 12:1–18:22

Deut 12:1–14

Here begins the law-code proper which goes on till 28 :
69, where it ends with much the same words as it here
begins. In 2 Kgs 22 : 8 there is an account of a law-book
being found when the temple was being repaired, which
became the basis of Josiah's reform and which seems to
have been the law-book of Deuteronomy, probably in an
earlier and shorter edition than the one we have in front
of us. At least the stipulations we shall now be reading
correspond rather exactly to the reform measures which
the young king carried through. We should also note that
this law-code is a follow-up and revision of that found in
Ex 20 : 22–23 : 33, which comes from the northern tribes.
In neither case are the laws laid down once for all; they
are a response to changing social, economic, and cultural
conditions. Many of them, therefore, such as the prohibition of boiling kids in their mothers' milk, will not be
of burning actuality for us today. We shall try in what
follows to pick out what is still in one way or another
relevant.

The first law, and certainly the most important, is the
insistence (three times) on unity of worship. This was
also the basis of Josiah's reform (see 2 Kgs 23 : 4). Disunity
had characterised all of Israel's history from the earliest

days. This had been tolerated, but the will of God for Israel is absolute unity based on one united worship and the abolition of separate altars. Unity is not therefore just an abstract idea or a union of hearts and minds, but must find concrete expression in one place of worship, one sanctuary, one altar. We recall how, when Jeroboam set up his own kingdom in the North, the first thing he did was to set up separate sanctuaries and altars—'and this thing became a sin' (1 Kgs 12 : 28–30).

We should note how the one sanctuary is chosen by God 'to put his name and make his habitation there' (12 : 5, 11). For the Hebrew the name is the nature, the active presence; God himself *dwells* in the sanctuary. Here we have the beginning of new testament incarnational theology, for when John says of Christ 'he dwelt amongst us' (1 : 14) he is using a technical theological or liturgical term first given currency by Deuteronomy (cf Solomon's prayer in the deuteronomic history 1 Kgs 8 : 27–29). The temple-saying in John ('he spoke of the temple of his body') transfers this incarnational idea from a building or sanctuary to the community; for the body of Christ here is not just the physical or eucharistic body but the body which is the church.

1.What light does the insistence on liturgical unity as the basis of a lived unity throw on our divided christian condition today?

2. In what way could we describe our disunited state as the result of sin, as the deuteronomic historian did in the case of the divided Israel?

Deut 12:15–28

This section legislates on what may or may not be eaten

locally and therefore can be disposed of rapidly. We might note how Deuteronomy reduces the sacral element to a minimum in contrast to the priestly rules and regulations in this area which do not make exciting reading for us today (eg, in Lev 17:3 ff). The old blood tabu remained and was, as we know, still there in new testament times and long after. In this respect we have to go on to read the saying of Jesus on what defiles a man and the account of how this problem was settled once and for all after the quarrel at Antioch at the so-called Council of Jerusalem (Acts 15).

What truth is there in the priestly-levitical idea in the old testament of a special area of the sacred as distinct from the profane?

Deut 12:29–13:18

The trouble was that it was perfectly natural at that time for anyone changing his land of residence to 'enquire about their gods' since it was commonly accepted that the power of a particular god obtained only within his own sphere of jurisdiction. Naaman the Syrian even took some Israelite soil back home in order to be able to continue worshipping Yahweh—a naïve and touching gesture—and the exiles ask in Babylon: 'How can we sing the hymns of Yahweh in a foreign land?' (Ps 137). The present passage was written with knowledge of how deeply Canaanite practices had penetrated into and corroded the faith of Israel—even human sacrifice had been practised to the greater glory of Yahweh. This explains the extreme severity of the three case-laws in chapter 13. There is no room for sweet reasonableness here, any more than in the sayings of Jesus about the sources of scandal

or the harsh words of Paul about the false gospellers (Gal
1:6–9). Maybe this is something we in the church tend
to play down today.

*How should we understand scandal in the context of
our christian witness today?*

Deut 14:1–29

This is another chapter which can be read rapidly or
even skipped if time is limited. After the three casuistic
laws of the preceding chapters we have a series of concise
ritual laws which begin and end with a short homiletic
amplification so common in this book. What is forbidden
by the first law may be taking part in a Canaanite ritual
of lamentation for the dead god of the vegetation (the
word *mt* in Hebrew can mean a dead person or Mot the
vegetation-god). The last prohibition (21b) is also aimed
against this sort of thing since we now know that boiling
a kid in its mother's milk was part of a Canaanite ritual.
The tabu laws about clean and unclean animals could
also have arisen because of the use of certain animals in
pagan ritual or perhaps in some cases out of a purely
natural revulsion. It was bad luck that they were denied
sea-food, but the Hebrews had always been confirmed
landlubbers. The last section gives the rules for the pay-
ment of tithes. This was a concrete means of bringing
home to them that the land belonged to their God, that
they had to live not of themselves but of God's gracious
act in fulfilling his promise. We should note here (14:26)
and throughout the insistence on *joy* in their liturgical
assemblies. The liturgy wasn't something 'spiritual' and
therefore solemn and rarified; it was a thoroughly human

act which those who took part in enjoyed, and nothing has happened since to change that.

Bearing in mind the number of times Deuteronomy insists on joy in the liturgical assembly, and the fact that the charismatic gifts were exercised in the early church during the service, what can we do to improve on our sometimes lugubrious liturgical practice?

Deut 15:1–23

The way Deuteronomy interprets the old law of leaving your crops ungathered every seventh year so that the poor could help themselves shows its concern for social action and collective responsibility. We find a great concern to legislate for the deprived classes which we have learnt to realise is still very much necessary in our affluent western society. Since it is likely that Deuteronomy was addressed primarily to the rather well-off landed classes who were behind the conservative reform of Josiah, this shows that the radical attack on social irresponsibility of the eighth-century prophets—Amos in particular—had borne some fruit. Not only is the law of the seventh-year release enunciated—there is also a clause against wangling out of it by legalistic quibbles (15:9). There follows a rule designed to protect those unfortunate people who had fallen foul of their creditors and had been sold into temporary slavery. The need for this kind of protection can be seen in Amos' complaint that 'they sell the righteous for silver, the pauper for a pair of sandals' (2:6). As always, of course, we have to see this concern of the writer against the social background of that time. Slavery, for example, was a sociological fact the need for which no one questioned either then, or in new testament times ('slaves, be obedient to your masters!' Eph 6:5), or for many centuries after. Where we might find cause for complaint here (as elsewhere in Deuteronomy) is in that suggestion of chauvinism and rather prickly nationalism which even survived the purification of the exile and was to play such a large part in distorting the old canonical community-idea up to the time of Christ.

The last few verses speak of the offering of the first-born of animals which was doubtless accompanied by the ancient liturgical formula we find in Ex 13:14–15, similar to the offering of the first sheaf of the harvest mentioned later in Deuteronomy.

1. How can christianity be regarded as a religion of social revolution when the revolutionary note seems to be conspicuous by its absence in both the old and new testaments?

2. For Deuteronomy the social and religious structure are identical. This is of course no longer the case but we may ask whether our structures—diocese and parish in particular—correspond to sociological realities and facilitate or impede the social mission of the church?

Deut 16:1–17

What follows is a kind of calendar of the three pilgrim festivals (there is only one word in Hebrew for 'feast' and 'pilgrimage'). Passover, Weeks, and Tents were all originally Canaanite festivals which the Hebrews took over from the people of the land—together with many other things, including their language—and historicised. Passover is referred to the Exodus, Weeks, later called Pentecost, to the giving of the law, and Tents was the autumn new year feast of covenant-renewal. Our christian celebration of Easter follows the passover-pattern: it is the solemn assembly, it is the feast of remembrance seen in the choice of scripture readings, and it is the feast of renewal. Weeks was the wheat-harvest festival in which God is celebrated as the giver, preparing for the christian feast of the Holy Spirit. Tents, corresponding to the autumn new year, was in Canaan, and later in Israel, the great festival of joy which sometimes tended to get out of hand, as a reading of Jgs 21:19 ff and 1 Sam 1 will show.

Christians still have feastdays and some of them even processions, but are we sure what purpose they have in the life of the local community? In Israel they were intimately linked with the realities of the everyday life of an agrarian community—the offering of the first-born and firstfruits with appropriate prayers—but we may be led to ask whether this purpose and relevance have survived the emergence of an urban and suburban civilisation in which people have only the shallowest of roots. Are feastdays and professions condemned to go the way of the harvest festival now that there are no more harvests?

1. Is our christian calendar of festivals calculated to survive in the industrial and technological age?
2. Are processions pointless?

Deut 16:18–18:22

There is a great deal of interest for us in this long section. It deals with offices or ministries within the nation-church, and chiefly with judges, the monarchy, the levitical priesthood and prophets. We realise, of course, that in the Israel in question here there was no division between

political and religious, secular and sacred, and that therefore a situation obtained different from that of the
modern church in a pluralist society. The organs of
justice and of executive rule are no longer christian
'ministries' even though what we find here could apply
to an individual christian judge or ruler. It is no longer
even practicable as a rule for christians to follow Paul's
advice and settle their differences out of court (1 Cor 6).
This section, however, gives a good insight into the tens-
ions inside the community between office and charism
and shows some of the dangers which attack the community-idea from within.

Without justice no community life is possible and in
fact no life at all is really worth living. There are norms
for the practice of justice. There is the ruling which insists on two or three witnesses both here and in 19:15–21,
which deals with perjury. In the absence of a police force
and any machinery for crime-detection the role of witnesses was crucial and had to be carefully controlled.
Ordinary cases were decided according to the old pattern,
by the tribal elders on the spot. Special cases and cases
of appeal were referred to a panel of levitical priests and
a judge.

It is significant that the monarchy comes under the
heading of community-ministries—Deuteronomy has no
time for any form of absolutised authority and would
have found a doctrine of divine right of kings distinctly
distasteful. The king falls under the covenant like anyone
else and is ruled by the same law and judged by the same
standard—he was to have 'a copy of this law' continually
by him (17:18, the Greek mistranslation of this phrase
gives us 'Deuteronomy'). Just as Israel, and the church
after it, cannot be viewed as a secular organisation with
rulers and ruled and the rest, so the king cannot be like

other kings. Status symbols such as the royal harem are to be avoided and there is that odd phrase about 'multiplying horses'—the horse for the camel- and donkey-using Hebrew was the war-engine *par excellence*.

The levitical priests (18:1–8) are first of all cult-functionaries whose job is the upkeep of the national sanctuary and who have the right to be supported by the rest of the population. In the old testament in general the priestly ministry is ideally an embodiment of the priestly function of the whole people, but already in Deuteronomy we see how the tension between this idea and that of a priestly caste could be broken in favour of the latter, which is unfortunately what happened. One symptom is that here provision is made for integrating the country priests, especially those from the separatist northern kingdom, into the Jerusalem ministry, but from the account of Josiah's religious reform (2 Kgs 23:9) we learn that the Jerusalem priests would have none of this. This question of the place of a priesthood within the christian community is still a problem for many today.

Deuteronomy is the heir of the northern tradition which sees prophecy as the chief manifestation of the Spirit which vitalises and dynamises the community and is the vital force running through the whole history of Israel. This last section (18:9–22) deals with the all-important question of the community's life-link with God. This is established by prophecy, the long, unbroken line of prophetic witness which continues the work of mediation of Moses, since we have to interpret the 'prophet like Moses' not in the first place of an individual but of the prophetic ministry as a whole. It is the prophet not the cult-functionary who mediates the word of God —'I will put my words in his mouth', those words by listening to which the community lives. When we read the list of surrogates for this which existed in Canaan, where ecstatic prophets were common, we might think of some modern varieties such as spiritualism and pentecostalism. In view of future developments in the history of Israel we should take careful note of the many indications we find in this book of Israel as a prophetic community. The 'prophet like Moses' is given an eschatological interpretation in later judaism as is clear from texts such as Jn 1:21 and the Qumran community rule. It was inevitable that it should be applied to Jesus by the early church since he was seen as a prophet as the community which he founded was prophetic.

One last point of interest. Among the laws in the rather abstrusive section 16:21–17:7 we find the prohibition of setting up a fertility goddess (Asherah) side by side with the altar which represents Yahweh. That there was good reason for this ruling we can see from the fact that Manasseh did just that (2 Kgs 21:7) and the statue was still there at the time of Ezekiel's conducted tour of the temple (Ezek 8:3). The religion of Israel went against the grain since its deity, unlike all other peoples' at that time, was uncompromisingly male and there was continual pressure to introduce the female principle into religious belief and practice. So we find, for example, that the Jewish colony at Assuan in Egypt worshipped both Yahweh and Anath the fertility-goddess side by side. Jung has some interesting things to say about the strong male character of christianity and the sometimes not too subtle ways in which this has been in practice if not in theory (that is, theology) modified. We can only speculate whether the centuries-long fight of Yahwism against a fertility religion has not left something of a scar on christianity with special reference to christian attitudes to sexuality.

1. How is office to be exercised within the church?

2. Have we really come to grips with the place of the ordained priest in the community? Is he to be merely a cult-functionary? What other roles should he play?

3. To what extent is christianity still in some respects, like the old-testament church, a man's religion?

6

Social responsibility and sexual conduct
Deut 19:1–26:15

Deut 19:1–21

The provision of cities of refuge, already alluded to, is an interesting case of the state gradually taking over the execution of justice from the blood-group as had been the case from time immemorial. Note, however, the careful distinction between homicide with malice aforethought and manslaughter. Communities in antiquity, which were organised according to kinship groups, and did not have a police force, relied entirely on group-responsibility for the detection and punishment of crime. The so-called law of retaliation (19:21), far from being a typical case of old testament barbarity, was an attempt to apply equity to the sometimes indiscriminate use of group-vengeance. It in its turn as to be superseded by Christ's command not to resist one who is evil (Mt 5:38–39) though we might wonder how seriously this has been taken in our christian history. In the same way, the over-riding need for justice expressed in the prophets and in the cursing psalms was to be modified by the claims of compassion and intercession for wrong-doing. Israel had still a lot to learn.

What ought to be the christian attitude to punishment?

Deut 20:1–20

We need spend little time on this chapter since we have already dealt with the holy war, an ideal very much theologised for Deuteronomy, as we saw, but which even when theologised as much as you like was swept away in the christian revelation. Of the idealised holy war at the end of time which we find in the Qumran war scroll there is no trace in the new testament, unless we interpret the mysterious saying of Jesus about selling one's cloak to buy a sword in that sense (Lk 22:36). For the record, this chapter lists cases of exemption from military service and mitigations of the original application of the 'ban'. But even when mitigated it doesn't make nice reading.

Presuming that there can no longer be such a thing as a holy war, where does this leave the christian with regard to military service?

Deut 21:1–22:12

In this section we find various prescriptions answering to the sociological conditions of the age but which are mostly of historical interest for us. The procedure in the event of undetected murder (21:1–9) seems to have been based on Canaanite custom and contains a considerable admixture of magic. The mandatory prayer, however, gives us a good insight into Israelite piety, addressing God as the redeemer of his people. The treatment of women prisoners-of-war, though a great advance on the practice in other lands, makes unpleasant reading, but that is also true of the permissive attitude to divorce in general. There follow three case-laws ('If a man . . .') dealing with safeguarding the observance of primogeniture in the case of polygamous marriage, the execution of a recalcitrant son, and the treatment of the corpse of an executed criminal whose body had been exposed, after execution, *pour encourager les autres*. The first part of chapter 22 has a bundle of laws, some of them humanitarian in character, others concerned with cultic irregularities, things which bring bad luck. In these latter there is often a magical idea which escapes us now, but the prohibition of transvestism may have something to do with obscene rites in Canaan. Let it be said once and for all that laws such as we find here have no absolute significance, much less binding force, in themselves apart from their documenting the history of the sacred community at one particular (and imperfect) stage of its development. Otherwise we may find ourselves emulating Calvin at Geneva and having children executed for lack of filial piety. We may be thankful that oracular exegesis is now practically extinct.

Reading some of these now obsolete laws raises the question of oracular exegesis since there have been people who thought we ought still to apply them where possible. Where is this kind of fundamentalism still with us?

Deut 22:13–30 and 24:1–4

There is a certain ambivalence or paradox about the whole old testament attitude to sex and sexual morality: detailed levitical rules of ritual purity and impurity at one end of the scale, the Song of Songs at the other; fairly easy-going attitude to divorce and polygamy at one end, severity with which the marriage bond was protected at the other. There is a long ruling here which deals with an allegation of infidelity made by a discontented husband against his wife with reference to the period of betrothal, which was taken far more seriously than is the case with us. If it is proved that she was unfaithful she is to be executed, but if his allegation is unfounded he suffers the penalty of a flogging and a heavy fine, with which we can compare the much heavier penalties imposed for the same thing in Assyria and elsewhere. Interesting this absolute exclusion of pre-marital sex—but was this due to the inherent holiness of the marriage bond or to insistence on the rights of the future husband? We have to bear in mind that throughout most of the old testament period the patriarchal view of marriage prevailed, and that this is quite different from our modern idea of partnership.

Adultery is punishable by death for both parties. The death penalty is also imposed for the rape of a betrothed girl—for the reason suggested above, namely, the rights of the future husband. 22:30 is not aimed at incest but at possessing one of the father's concubines, which is what two of David's sons attempted to do. We can conveniently anticipate here our reading of the prohibition of re-marriage with the same woman after she has been divorced from another man (in 24:1-4, we still read of it happening now and again) if only to point out that Vulgate has misunderstood it as a divorce law which it isn't; the divorced woman has now become *tabu* for her first husband for reasons which will hardly interest us today. When they tried to draw Jesus into the Shammai-Hillel row about what constituted sufficient reason for divorce, he naturally brushed aside the appeal to this text as irrelevant and went back to first principles.

1. How must our changed view of marriage as a partnership affect our scriptural reading with regard to both old- and new-testament teaching on sexual morality?

2. What reflections do our reading of passages such as this provoke on the relevance of 'natural law' arguments in this sphere?

3. If it is true that Jesus did not lay down absolute laws apart from the one law of love, what about the prohibition of divorce with or without the exceptive clause? Why do we give it a privileged interpretation if, for example, his even more absolute prohibition of swearing oaths does not prevent us doing so in a court of law?

Deut 23:1–25

The chapter begins with cultic disqualifications for taking part in the great annual tribal assembly, the 'church of Israel'. They are either physical or ethnic in character; the 'bastard' in question was probably a descendant of the hybrid population of Philistia and is a limbering up for the crude slanging match between Jew and Gentile around the time of Christ and Paul. This exclusivism began to fade with the realisation of Israel's world-mission. The post-exilic Isaiah admits both eunuchs and foreigners to Israel (56:3–4) and we have an instructive contrast between the Qumran community, which applied similar restrictions for membership of their group, and the words of Jesus about the halt and the lame entering the kingdom. The ritual laws for purity in 'the camp' (9–14) need not detain us nor the laws in favour of runaway slaves, against cult-prostitutes and lending at interest to fellow-Israelites which follow. This last played its part in the mediaeval condemnation of usury.

How should we apply the absolute christian rejection of exclusivism today?

Deut 24:5–25:4

One remarkable thing about the Deuteronomic code is its attempt to get people to waive their strictly legal rights in the interests of the deprived classes. It may all look pretty primitive to us reading these laws after more than two and a half millennia and judging them from our superior position of advantage, but that may be due to our lack of imaginative insight. In this section, for example, there are rules relating to taking pledges for debts owed. The pledge mustn't be seized; wait outside for him to bring you it. There are rules, or better, exhortations, to leave something after harvesting for the needy. There is also the insistence on paying casual labourers the same day. Enslaving an insolvent debtor—a thing common in other countries—was punishable by death. There are strict rules against the imposition of excessively degrading punishments and the number of strokes in a whipping was not to exceed forty—later the 'forty stripes save one' administered to Paul.

We might easily miss the principle enunciated in 24 : 16 which concludes: 'Every man shall be put to death for his own sin.' Here we can see a juridical principle evolving into a theological statement—that of personal responsibility. Worked out during the exilic period when the problems of responsibility and providence were particularly acute (see Jer 31 : 29 and especially Ezek 18) it modified and corrected the old idea of communal responsibility which was thought of as operating both vertically (father to son) and horizontally (within the blood group). This brought nearer the possibility of thinking of a future condition of reward and punishment after death.

1. What more should christians be doing for the de-

prived classes of our own day and, in particular, in our own welfare-state?

2. *What meaning has the biblical idea of group-respon-sibility in the changed circumstances of today?*

Deut 25:4–19

What is described here and generally known as the levir-ate law (from Latin *levir* = brother-in-law) was fairly common in the ancient Near East and practised by peoples as far apart as Hittites and Yemeni Arabs. The idea was to keep together the family inheritance, which was important even though the means adopted must seem rather odd to us. One recalls that Onan son of Judah died as a result of refusing his social responsibilities in this respect (Gen 38:6 ff) and there is another case in Ruth 4 which illustrates very well some aspects of what we read here. The custom gradually weakened and dis-appeared, though there are still traces of it in new testa-ment times (see Mt 22:23 ff).

In the law immediately following we have the only case of mutilation ever practised in Israel. The insistence on correct weights and measures reflects the bitter campaign for social justice waged by the prophets, who didn't stay on the level of lofty generalisation as a glance at passages such as the following will prove: Am 8:5; Hos 12:8–9; Mic 6:10–12.

Fighting for social justice often means taking sides. Can we decide on which side to fight on the basis of social commitment alone?

Deut 26:1–15

The offering of the firstfruits and the accompanying

prayer form one of the most important passages in Deuteronomy and indeed in the whole of the old testament. They show us something original and irreducible: a glimpse through the depths of theological and traditional overlay of a Hebrew going to the central sanctuary of the tribes on one of the great festivals with his sheaf of barley to offer it to God as an acknowledgement of dependence and a sign of self-offering, reciting the ancient words fixed by tradition for this occasion. The occasion was probably Azymes, taken over from the Canaanites but charged with a new religious meaning expressed in the confession of faith (or 'cultic credo', von Rad) which he made.

The words of the confession convey a tremendous sense of *participation*—a key word for Hebrew religious faith. My father Jacob (renamed Israel) went down into Egypt; he became a great nation; the Egyptians treated *us* harshly. My father was in Egypt and he was Israel; therefore I too was afflicted and in grievous bondage. In virtue of this the land has been given as a promise fulfilled after many years. The offering of the firstfruits is the offering of the good land back to the giver, an abjuration of life lived *of and to oneself*: 'And behold, now I bring the first of the fruit of the ground which thou, O Lord, hast given me.'

Here we are at the liturgical roots of the historical tradition of the Pentateuch (or Hexateuch). If we turn to Josh 24, the covenant-festival at Shechem, we find that another concentric circle has been added and the liturgical memory has gone further back, to Abraham. This tells us something about the relations between liturgy and doctrine and why our central statement of faith is also essentially a historical recital first elaborated by means of liturgical usage.

The final bit about the distribution of tithes has also preserved an old liturgical formula and we have another example of Hebrew piety in the prayer with which it concludes.

1. Harvest festivals are all right for people who live in the country. What equivalent is there for the rest of us?
2. How can we experience this participation in a common past, this belonging to one prophetic community which continues from one age to the next?

7

The sealing of the covenant
Deut 26:16–31:1

Deut 26:16–27:26

The public reading of the covenant law is finished and the parties seal their mutual commitment with a solemn declaration (26:17, 18). The covenant-statement made by Yahweh is very simple and compendious: 'I will be your God and you will be my people' which makes us understand how Hosea could call his last child *Lo-ammi*, Not-my-people, 'for you are not my people and I am not your God' (Hos 1:9), and how the people of the new covenant —ourselves—could be addressed: 'Once you were no-people but now you are God's people' (1 Pet 2:10).

Covenants were usually sealed with a ceremony which included some or all of the following actions: setting up an altar or commemorative monument, offering sacrifice and sharing in a sacrificial meal, writing or engraving the stipulations and putting them in or near a sanctuary, pronouncing a list of curses and blessings (sometimes just curses) which the contracting parties took upon themselves to secure their mutual fidelity. Chapters 27 and 28 refer to most of these actions but in a rather mixed-up way since at least two covenant traditions have been not too skilfully conflated. In reading them we should note how deeply the covenant idea has influenced the new testament, beginning with Jesus himself. 'New testament'

means new covenant, the eucharist is a covenant meal—
at once a service of remembrance and a sealing of the
community's commitment (cf Ex 24:8, 'Behold the blood
of the covenant which the Lord has made with you' and
Mt 26:28, 'Behold my blood of the covenant which is
poured out for many.'). Other covenant features in the
new testament we can leave to discussion. One is suggested by a comparison between the ceremony at Shechem, which is on the plain between two hills, and Luke's
sermon on the plain (Lk 6:20 ff).

*1. How does Deuteronomy help us to understand what
it means to belong to the people of God?*

*2. How can we express the covenant-idea in a way fully
intelligible to our contemporaries today?*

Deut 28:1–68

This is certainly one of the longest chapters in the bible
but hardly one of the most interesting. It contains the
blessings and curses of the original deuteronomic covenant, and if cursing takes up much more space than blessing we have to remember that cursing was really more
important, as being the self-administered covenant-oath,
meant as a form of self-binding and commitment. Interesting to note that none of the curses pursue the cursed
after death—with the exception of that of remaining un-
buried. In the judgement-scene in Mt 25 referred to
earlier, the blessing and curse take in the future life. The
curses reflect real experience and lead up to a climax of
horror in the description of cannibalism within the be-
sieged capital. They also portray the destiny of the chosen
people in reverse like a film shown backwards: they are
driven out of the land, back into the desert, and thence

into Egypt where they suffer the same plagues that the Lord had inflicted on their oppressors. Israel is back where she started. The chapter ends with an impression-istic account of life in exile in Babylon.

Reading this chapter, and many others in the old testa-ment, we see how total faith and commitment were con-sistent with the absence of any thought of a life after death. How has our obsession with rewards and punish-ments in a future life distorted our grasp of christian essentials?

Deut 29:1–29

Now that the covenant ceremony is complete we have another homily summarising the Moab covenant-renewal and attributed to Moses. Typically, however, the writer soon forgets this and by 29:6 it is the Lord himself who is speaking, he whose self-revelation is at the centre of the covenant. Since for christians this self-disclosing has its final and definitive form in Christ we can see how covenant and incarnation go together and why there are so many covenant-motifs in the new testament (examples from this chapter which can be looked into privately: 29: 18, cf Heb 6:12; 29:19; cf Lk 23:31; 29:29, cf Mt 11:27).

We can best read the chapter by dividing it into two parts: 29:1–15 is a real covenant-text, though of course worked over: 'all-Israel' is a technical term for the plen-ary liturgical assembly, the people are *standing* (29:10) as people ought to at a liturgical gathering, and there is the strong theme of remembrance, collective memory, which is the cement of unity. The rest of the chapter has been added on by a preacher during the Babylonian exile and is largely directed against the danger of idolatry in the same way as one can see in the poems of the great anonymous prophet of the exile in Is 40 ff.

How can our study of the covenant help us to understand the place of Christ?

Deut 30:1–31:1

This chapter too must come from near the end of the period of exile and seems to have been influenced by the promise of a new covenant in Jeremiah (31:31–34), a passage which should be re-read at this point. The exile had meant a great crisis of faith. For the first time the church of Israel came in contact with the world and, as it happened, a world in the throes of a deep and lasting transformation. It was the age of the *oikoumene* represented by the worldwide Persian empire, the age when the mythical system was beginning to break up, of the Ionian philosophers, of Zoroaster, Buddha, and Confucius. A national god waging his little local wars was too small for a world like that. The solid national 'church' had become a dispersion church, small communities trying to hold on as best they could in a hostile or indifferent environment. How could Israel survive and carry out her mission? For that matter, what *was* her mission?

One part of the answer is to be found in the servant songs of Isaiah written in or near this period; the hardest part, that of unrewarded service, and one which had and has to be continually relearnt. The other is in this chapter. Israel must *return* to the Lord (note the play on the dual meaning of conversion and physical return to the land of promise). Israel must live by God's word proclaimed to her in the liturgical service. 30:11–14, about

God who comes near through his word, are one of the high moments of old testament religious thinking. Through his word God is no longer 'up there' or 'over there' but *here*, wherever there is a community ready to listen. It is not difficult to see how we are now approaching nearer to the biblical understanding of what christian theologians call the incarnation, the mystery of the incarnate word.

The homily ends with a recall to the basic covenant-idea of decision and commitment in the form of the two ways (life—death, good—evil, blessing—curse) which is found at Qumran and in early christian writings. In this it resembles early christian preaching, ending not with credal statements or theological reflections but with a call to decision: Choose life! (30:19), Repent and believe the good news!

As we now see from a Qumran biblical fragment, 31:1 should read 'Moses finished speaking these words' and is therefore a conclusion, not an introduction.

1. How has 'the world' and our commitment to the world made us see the church in a new light? To what extent have we preserved the tension between commitment and separation?

2. How can a modern man, truly living in the world, not be an atheist?

8

Last words and death of Moses
Deut 31:2–34:12

Deut 31:2–30

Whether or not the bible is the worst printed book in the world, as has been claimed, it certainly is the worst edited. This chapter is a good example, since it contains three themes mixed up in a way which seems downright perverse. One is the succession of Joshua, important since it indicates the charismatic nature not only of office but of succession to office in the holy community. We shall later read that 'Joshua was full of the spirit of wisdom for Moses had laid his hands upon him' (34:9) and the fuller account in Num 11:16–30 brings this out even more clearly. One could read consecutively as follows: 31:14–15, 2–3, 7–8, 23. Then there is the normal winding up of a covenant-ceremony with the command to write out the stipulations, put them in the sanctuary (here, near the ark) and have them read out to the assembled covenant-people at regular intervals—here, every seven years. Read 31:9–13, 24–27. Later on, someone added on the hymn of Moses, which is much older than the framework in which it is now found, which was to be a witness against the Israelites by stirring up their memories and consciences. The introduction to this liturgical hymn is in 31:16–22, 28–30.

What light does the account of Joshua succeeding to Moses throw on what we mean by ordination?

Deut 32:1–44

This old hymn, despite its length, well deserves a reading. Couched in the vivid colours of Canaanite mythological poetry, the imagery of the high-god El and his heavenly court, of the fertile earth and Yahweh as the 'rider on the clouds', it cannot fail to appeal to anyone open to this kind of language. It was evidently fitted into Deuteronomy because it illustrated the central theme of choice and rejection and who he is with whom the people enter into relationship: 'I, even I, am he, and there is no god beside me!' (32 : 39, the climax of the poem). He is not a dying and rising god but one that 'kills and makes alive', the living and life-giving God. Reading it and remembering its liturgical function as a 'witness', we might be led to some rueful reflections on the kind of hymns we latterday Israelites sing and the whole function of hymn-singing in the liturgy, which is perhaps the most neglected element of recent liturgical reform.

1. What is the function of the hymn in the liturgy?
2. What should be our attitude to hymn-singing?

Deut 32:45–34:12

Once the hymn is finished, we have Moses' last exhortation to keep the law which is to be their *life*. How then could Paul say that the same law was death-dealing? If law is understood outside of the context of the covenant, as a system or a code in itself, it could and did bring death, and it is tragic how common it still is to hear christianity described as a code. This, however, takes us beyond the limits of our study. The account of the last days and death of Moses the prophet continues into chapter 34 which is also, we should remember, the conclusion to the whole Pentateuch or *torah*. From mount Nebo one can, on a clear day, see the low line of the Mediterranean in the distance, and the panorama described here takes in an immense ark from north to south. There is a moment of genuine pathos as the old man looks out with undimmed eye over the good land he was not to enter. And since his end could hardly be less numinous than that of Elijah, *God buried him* and no one to this day knows where. Since also it was customary to attribute 'famous last words' to the great, as with Jacob and David, we find Moses blessing the twelve tribes in the person of their ancestors before he dies.

What have we still to learn from Deuteronomy's presentation of law as a gift and a blessing?